MONARCHY
BEHIND THE SCENES WITH
THE ROYAL FAMILY

MONARCHY
BEHIND THE SCENES WITH
THE ROYAL FAMILY

St. Martin's Press
New York

Picture Credits

All photographs by Tim Graham, except: The Queen on horseback during the sovereign's Birthday Parade, and the Princess of Wales and her sons on the steps of one of The Queen's Flight aeroplanes; both by Rex Features.

MONARCHY. Copyright © 1987 by Brian Hoey. All rights reserved. Printed in the United States of America. No part of this book may be used or reproduced in any manner whatsoever without written permission except in the case of brief quotations in critical articles or reviews. For information, address St. Martin's Press, 175 Fifth Avenue, New York, N.Y. 10010.

Library of Congress Cataloging-in-Publication Data

Hoey, Brian.
    Monarchy : behind the scenes with the royal family / by Brian
Hoey.
    p   cm.
    ISBN 0-312-01475-9 : $15.95
    1. Elizabeth II, Queen of Great Britain, 1926– —Family.
2. Great Britain—Kings and rulers—Biography. 3. Great Britain-
-Princes and princesses—Biography. 4. Monarch—Great Britain-
-History—20th century. I. Title.
DA590.H6 1988
941.085′092′4—dc19
[B]   87-27950
                                             CIP

First published in Great Britain by BBC Books.

First U.S. Edition

10 9 8 7 6 5 4 3 2 1

CONTENTS

INTRODUCTION

The idea for this book originated with a radio programme, or rather, a series of radio programmes. In January 1985 I had been discussing with Michael Shea, The Queen's Press Secretary, a number of possible ways in which the BBC could mark the occasion of Her Majesty's sixtieth birthday on 21 April 1986. It was finally agreed that we should mount eight radio programmes, to be broadcast on Radio Four, which would attempt to explain some of the mysteries surrounding the monarchy. For instance, how much power does the sovereign really have in a constitutional monarchy? Who owns the Crown Jewels and how much are they actually worth? What really goes on when The Queen and the Prime Minister meet for their weekly discussion on Tuesday evenings? Are the leaders of the Commonwealth in favour of having an hereditary monarch as their Head?

Among other things, we looked at the relationship between Parliament and the monarchy; we talked to former Prime Ministers such as Lord Home, Lord Wilson and James Callaghan. The Archbishop of Canterbury gave his views on the relevance of The Queen's role as Defender of the Faith in this latter part of the twentieth century, while Lord Soper (a staunch republican) argued that the monarchy is an anachronism in this day and age.

The production team was given a unique insight into the workings of the monarchy, so much so that we ended up with far more material than we were able to include in the total of four hours' programme time available to us. We went behind the scenes at Buckingham Palace and Windsor Castle; we saw the treasures of the Royal Collection through the eyes of Sir Oliver Millar, Surveyor of The Queen's Pictures; and we were guided through the Private Apartments of the Royal Yacht *Britannia*, by The Queen's Steward. The same access was granted when we went to visit The Queen's Flight at RAF Benson in Oxfordshire – nothing was denied us; we could go anywhere and talk to anyone without any form of censorship.

So what this book aims to do, in common with the radio series, is present the most comprehensive explanation of Britain's Royal Family today; its constitutional role and its historical perspective. By talking to members of the Royal Household and, more significantly, to members of the Royal Family, we were able to look not only at the way history has recorded the events which mark the milestones in our monarchy, but also at the way in which those who play both the major and minor roles regard themselves.

This is not an authorised biography of the Royal Family and no part of the book has been subjected to any form of scrutiny by anyone in the Royal Household, so any opinions offered are mine alone, unless they are from quoted sources. I do, however, have to confess at this point to a bias towards the subject. I am in favour of the monarchy and the first opinion I will venture is this: I suspect the majority of the British people wish to keep their monarchy and many people in other parts of the world (even those to whom the idea of being ruled by an hereditary Head of State is anathema) are nevertheless fascinated by ours.

Brian Hoey

THE MONARCHY TODAY

In the early hours of 6 February 1952, King George VI died in his sleep and his daughter Elizabeth became Queen. At twenty-five years of age, she became the forty-second sovereign of England since William the Conqueror, yet only its sixth Queen Regnant, ruling in her own right. The monarchy is Britain's oldest secular institution. It pre-dates Parliament by 400 years and the law courts by 300. The Queen can trace her descent, through the hereditary principle, in direct line from King Egbert, the first Monarch of All England in 829. In 1000 years the continuity of the British monarchy has been broken only once: in the seventeenth century, when the republic of Oliver Cromwell ruled from 1649–1660.

Her Majesty's full titles, which were accorded her at her coronation in Westminster Abbey on 2 June 1953, are: Elizabeth the Second, by the Grace of God, of the United Kingdom of Great Britain and Northern Ireland, and of her other Realms and Territories Queen, Head of the Commonwealth, Defender of the Faith. This last description might seem to be somewhat archaic in a country where only one person in twenty professes to be a Christian and in a Commonwealth with a population of over 900 million, more than half of whom are certainly not of the Christian faith. However, the present Archbishop of Canterbury, Dr Robert Runcie, has no reservations about this aspect of The Queen's role in public life:

In the strict legal sense of the phrase, the Copyright Act of 1958 gives to The Queen, as part of the royal prerogative, the sole right of printing and licensing others to print the authorised version of the Bible and the Book of Common Prayer. So this means there is a responsibility on the part of the sovereign to protect access to the Bible and the Book of Common Prayer for Christians, which have been described as the two pillars of the Reformation settlement in England.

Dr Runcie also sees the relevance of the title Defender of the Faith as being apposite to the way in which The Queen acts and speaks personally. He says, 'She is perceived as someone whose dedication to God at her coronation, and her anointing for Christian service to her people, colours the whole exercise of her office.'

The man who has been closer to the sovereign than anyone else for nearly forty years, the Duke of Edinburgh, also has definite ideas of the value of having a monarch as Head of State:

9

The advantage of a monarchy is that it doesn't enter into the political arguments of the day. It makes for a very good division of responsibilities; the Prime Minister does all the political business and this means that those people who oppose him politically don't have to oppose him as Head of State. The monarchy is above politics.

The last Queen Regnant was our present Queen's great-great-grandmother, Queen Victoria, who reigned over one of the greatest empires ever known. Britain's pre-eminence in trade and industry made her the most powerful nation in the world and her monarch the most envied on earth. Britain's influence as a world power has diminished considerably in the eighty-five years since Victoria's death, but Elizabeth II has retained and even increased the admiration and respect that was once reserved for only the world's strongest and most powerful leaders. The British monarchy may well have lost many of its awesome powers of authority, but it has retained a dignity and dedication which it is impossible to deny. And Elizabeth II, who has accepted with grace the changed circumstances of a once all-powerful position, has enhanced the role of the modern sovereign, in part through her personal example as a down-to-earth, hard-working wife and mother. She extols the virtues of a Christian tradition in her own family life and she has managed to combine with distinction her public and private lives.

One of the Commonwealth's elder statesmen, President Kenneth Kaunda of Zambia, says, 'She is loved not because she is Queen and Head of the Commonwealth but because of who she is, first and foremost.' And Sir 'Sonny' Ramphal, Secretary-General of the Commonwealth, is equally emphatic about the personal qualities of Her Majesty:

There is no doubt in my mind, and I'm quite sure the minds of all the leaders of the Commonwealth countries – and there are forty-nine today – that The Queen occupies a unique position, which is unique because of who she is. She is the most experienced Head of State in the world; she regards many of the Commonwealth leaders as personal friends and even those who have only recently taken over the leadership of their countries look to her for guidance and advice. It doesn't make any difference if the countries are republics or not, they look upon The Queen as the one influence of continuity in an ever-changing world. And of course it's important to remember that four of the Commonwealth countries are monarchies in their own right: Lesotho, Malaysia, Swaziland and Tonga.

Elizabeth Alexandra Mary, the first child of Prince Albert and Elizabeth, Duke and Duchess of York, was born on 21 April 1926 in a private house at 17 Bruton Street, the home of her maternal grandparents, in the heart of London's West End. Shortly afterwards they moved to a comfortable house at 145 Piccadilly, a house which has long since been demolished, with not even a small plaque left on the wall of the hotel that replaced it to commemorate the fact that The Queen once lived there. For, happy though the incident of her birth was to her parents and indeed to her grandparents King George V and Queen Mary, there was no reason to regard the arrival of this little girl as a moment of any great significance. Her father was a second son who had no expectation or desire to inherit the throne. His elder brother David, Prince of Wales, was then only twenty-seven, and though he was still a bachelor, it was confidently anticipated that he would, in due course, make a suitable marriage and provide future heirs. So even though Elizabeth was third in line of succession at her birth, no one could foresee the events which would take place almost exactly ten years later, and which would propel her from comparative obscurity to the position of heir presumptive.

Elizabeth's father was a shy, introverted man who had suffered from being dominated in his youth by an excessively stern father. As a consequence he was to become a doting parent to both his first daughter Elizabeth and her sister Margaret Rose, who was born four years later. Prince Albert, known as Bertie, had spent five years as a naval officer, but even the discipline of Britain's senior service did not cure his innate nervousness which resulted in a pronounced stammer. This condition was never completely cured, but it was alleviated considerably by the sympathetic understanding of his wife, the former Lady Elizabeth Bowes-Lyon. Indeed, if the family had any 'news value' at that time, it was because of the popularity of this Duchess of York, who was regarded as one of the great beauties of the day, and who was affectionately called 'the little Duchess' by the public and the Press alike.

The first ten years of Elizabeth's life were spent in idyllic conditions. With homes in London and in the country, her family passed the seasons in the way that wealthy people had always passed them. The Duke and Duchess had certain public responsibilities, but they always managed to fit them in around their own family life and the two little Princesses probably saw more of their parents than many of their contemporaries. Neither of them went to school: their education was undertaken privately at home; something which did nothing to prevent The Queen from sending all four of her own children away to boarding school when the time came. But in 1936, events occurred which were to dramatically change not only the circumstances of this family but the history of Britain and the British monarchy. The story of Edward VIII, the uncrowned King of England, the man who gave up his throne and an empire for the woman he loved, has been chronicled time and time again. It was an episode which had its sad but final conclusion on Tuesday 29 April 1986, when the Duchess of Windsor was buried beside her husband in the royal vault at Frogmore in Windsor Great Park. Theirs was called 'the greatest love story of the century' and indeed it lasted for more than fifty years – all of which were spent in exile after the abdication.

David, Prince of Wales, was Elizabeth's favourite uncle. He epitomised all that was glamorous and romantic. As one of the world's most eligible bachelors he was sought after by all the leading society hostesses and he formed a number of liaisons with ladies of high birth or great wealth, who were almost invariably married. In 1931, however, he met the woman who was to dominate his life thereafter, and change the course of British history. Wallis Warfield Simpson and her husband, an American businessman, were fellow guests at a country house in Leicestershire when they were presented to the Prince. Almost from that day, Mrs Simpson, who had already been divorced once, became the most important influence in his life. He abandoned all his former girl-friends for his new love and even arranged for her to be presented at Court. Mr Simpson was aware of the attraction his wife held for the Prince from the beginning, but he raised no objections to their friendship and contented himself with being included in the royal party whenever convention demanded his presence. Wallis Simpson seemed an unusual choice as a companion for the Prince of Wales. He was used to the company of some of the richest and most attractive women in the world. Wallis came from a lower-middle-class background. She had no money of her own and physically she would never be classed as a beauty. But to the Prince she was complex and elusive. He described her as 'the most independent woman I have ever met' and very quickly became besotted with her, to the exclusion of everything else – including his royal duties.

By 1935, the year of King George V's Silver Jubilee, the Prince of Wales had made up his mind that he wanted to marry Wallis Simpson, even though she was at that time still married to her second husband. The Prince knew his father would disapprove of the marriage and indeed had the power to prevent it. Under the Royal Marriages Act of 1772, the marriages of Princes of the Blood Royal are under the sovereign's control (and, ultimately, Parliament's) so if the King used his power of veto that would be the end of it. The Prince never raised the topic with his father, partly because he knew the outcome and partly because the King, who had been in poor health for some time, was too ill to be bothered by such news. In January 1936 His Majesty died at Sandringham and David became King Edward VIII.

Edward was to reign for only eleven months and become known as 'the King who was never crowned'. (This is because the coronation of an incoming sovereign rarely takes place less than a year after the accession to the throne. In the first place there is the period of Court mourning, usually several months; then the new sovereign is involved in selecting his or her Household, which is always a lengthy procedure. Moreover, the preparations for a coronation take many months to arrange, with the temporary building work at Westminster Abbey and all the arrangements for foreign Heads of State and other dignitaries to be present.)

The new King was determined that Mrs Simpson would continue to be part of his life. She was invited to stay at Balmoral and other royal residences, and on the King's specific instructions her name was included in the Court Circular. This, however, was the only reference to her made in the British Press at the time. Because the King had already told the Prime Minister that he wanted to marry Mrs Simpson when her divorce came through, Baldwin had acted quickly to try and suppress any possible adverse Press comment about the King and a divorcee, wishing to avoid a national scandal. The Prime Minister was against the marriage from the beginning and told the King that neither the people nor the government would tolerate it. If the King persisted, he would have to abdicate. The King had his supporters, who urged him to ignore Baldwin. One of them was the Canadian newspaper magnate Lord Beaverbrook, owner of the *Daily Express*. He agreed not to publish any details of the 'Simpson Story' and prevailed upon his colleagues in Fleet Street to do the same. So throughout the period of the biggest constitutional crisis this century, the majority of the British people were kept in complete ignorance of a story that was being blasted all over the front pages of every newspaper in America and Europe. The self-imposed ban even extended to the divorce of Mrs Simpson, which took place at Ipswich Assizes on 27 October 1936. The newspapers reported the facts of the case and that was all, with no comment, interviews or editorial. The row between the King on the one hand and the government – as represented by Prime Minister Baldwin – on the other continued for several months, with each determined to have his way. The King refused to give up Mrs Simpson and the Prime Minister was equally adamant that a divorced woman was unacceptable as the wife of the sovereign. Eventually the matter was resolved when the King decided to abdicate in favour of his brother Bertie. The Duke of York was reluctant to accept the crown at first, having a shy and retiring nature and being happily married with two young daughters. He knew that his life and that of his family would change beyond all recognition, but when the time came for him to assume the responsibility of the throne, he accepted with dignity, subsequently becoming one of the best-loved sovereigns in British history.

When the abdication of Edward VIII was announced it was seen by the majority of the British people as a dereliction of duty, even though there were many who maintained that what he had done was to show that nothing is more important than love. The King's mother, Queen Mary, never forgave her son for what she regarded as an unforgivable breach of a sacred trust. History has recorded, however, that what seemed at first a selfish act on the part of a weak, self-indulgent man turned out to be the best thing that could possibly have happened to the British monarchy.

Princess Elizabeth of York had become heir presumptive and the British people, once they had come to terms with the fact of the abdication, immediately transferred their allegiance and affection to the new King, George VI, and his Family. It was quite remarkable, particularly because, as far as the general public was concerned, it had happened almost overnight. The media had managed to keep silent on the love affair and the constitutional crisis it presented for more than three years. When it eventually became known, and the abdication was a *fait accompli*, the British people accepted the accession of the King's younger brother Bertie totally – although it is significant that on the night of the abdication, live ammunition was issued to the sentries guarding Buckingham Palace for the first and only time.

When the time came for the coronation to take place, it was as if Edward VIII had never existed: even the day remained the same – only the name of the man who was to be crowned was changed. Royal historians have recorded that since that day, the abdication has never been mentioned in Court circles, and certainly the two Princesses were not encouraged to discuss their uncle David, the ex-king. It was also from the day of the coronation that Princess Elizabeth's training for her future role as sovereign began. At the ceremony itself she sat next to her grandmother Queen Mary, with her sister Princess Margaret, and it was Queen Mary who took it upon herself to help educate the future monarch in the years following the coronation. She insisted on dragging her granddaughters around such historic London landmarks as the Tower, the Royal Mint and Hampton Court, with rarely a thought as to whether they were enjoying themselves – only that they were learning something of the history and traditions of the land one of them would one day reign over.

The outbreak of the Second World War in September 1939 caused certain changes in the domestic routine of the Royal Family. The two Princesses were removed to Windsor Castle where they remained for the duration of hostilities and they saw the surrounding acres of parkland ploughed under to help provide food for the war effort. The King led by personal example, pushing himself physically and mentally to such an extent that his wife became worried about his ability to continue. But there was no question of a let-up. As long as he could see his subjects making sacrifices at home and abroad, the King felt it was imperative that he should also be seen to be working alongside them.

At the height of the blitz it was suggested to the Queen that she and her daughters should leave Britain for Canada. The suggestion received such little consideration that the answer given by Her Majesty has become one of the most famous of all wartime sayings: 'The children will not leave without me; I will not leave without the King; the King will never leave.' And of course they all remained in Britain throughout the war.

Princess Elizabeth joined the ATS (the Auxiliary Territorial Service) shortly before her nineteenth birthday in 1945. It was the culmination of the months of lobbying her father by the young Princess, who was anxious to 'do her bit' for the war effort. She was commissioned as a second subaltern and allocated a service number, which, like all other servicemen and women, she would remember for the rest of her life – 230873. She learnt how to drive and service heavy lorries and the only concession that was made to the daughter of the King, was that she was allowed to return to Windsor at night, rather than stay with her fellow officers at the transport depot at Camberley where she was stationed. Even this concession was granted at the request of His Majesty and not the Princess herself, who would have preferred to stay outside the Castle. But the King had enough anxieties at the time without worrying where his daughter was and so Princess Elizabeth complied with this 'bending of the rules'.

VE Day, 8 May 1945, was probably the last occasion when Princess Elizabeth was allowed to be 'one of the people' for a few hours. She joined the crowd outside the gates of Buckingham Palace who were calling for the King and Prime Minister Winston Churchill to appear on the balcony. At first the King was reluctant to allow his daughters to go outside the Palace because of the size of the crowds and the fear that they might be caught in the crush. However, as he later wrote in his diary: 'Poor darlings, they have never had any fun yet.' Hundreds of thousands of men, women and children and servicemen from all the allied countries had massed in The Mall dancing and singing and shouting over and over again for the King and Queen to appear on the balcony. Princess Elizabeth and Princess Margaret, with their uncle David Bowes-Lyon, 'Crawfie' their governess and a group of young officers, left the palace by a side entrance, worked their way around the back of St James's and into The Mall where they linked up with the rest of the crowd, who were dancing and shouting their heads off in the excitement of the moment. Nobody recognised them, or if they did, they probably didn't believe it was them. It was a brief moment of freedom that was over all too soon – and never to be repeated.

The Princess's twenty-first birthday, celebrated in South Africa on 21 April 1947, was significant for the speech she made which was broadcast to the world. In it she dedicated her future life to the service of the people she would shortly reign over:

I declare before you that my whole life, whether it be long or short, shall be devoted to your service and the service of our great Imperial Commonwealth to which we all belong. But I shall not have strength enough to carry out this resolution unless you join in it with me, as I now invite you to do; I know that your support will be unfailingly given. God bless all of you who are willing to share it.

Of course, the unconscious irony of the occasion lay in the place in which the speech was made, for South Africa was to be the first country in what was then the British Empire and Commonwealth to sever all connections with the British monarchy.

The year 1947 was to be of great moment in British history. India became independent and so all future British sovereigns would lose the right to be called Emperor; Princess Elizabeth became engaged to Lieutenant Philip Mountbatten and on 20 November that same year they were married in Westminster Abbey. It was a time of austerity during those early post-war years, with severe rationing still in force, but the bride was allowed extra clothing coupons to enable her to complete her trousseau. Clarence House, which had been empty for some years, became home for the royal couple and for five years, during which time two children, Prince Charles and Princess Anne, were born, Princess Elizabeth lived as a naval officer's wife. There were frequent absences abroad for the family, especially to Malta, where the Duke of Edinburgh was stationed for much of the time. Throughout this period the Princess was taking an ever-increasing share of royal duties in an effort to relieve the burden on the King's shoulders.

On 31 January 1952, King George VI saw his daughter off at London's Heathrow airport as she departed for the second part of an extended Commonwealth Tour. The King had been too ill to continue himself as he had wished and, as he bade farewell to his daughter on the draughty tarmac, there may well have been a thought in his mind that this could be the last time he would see her. On 6 February, within a week of leaving London, Princess Elizabeth heard of the death of her father. She was staying at Sagana Lodge in Nyeri National Park in Kenya, when Sir Martin Charteris, her Private Secretary, received word from Buckingham Palace and he informed the Duke of Edinburgh, who told his wife.

So the 25-year-old who had left Britain as a Princess, returned as Queen. The first person to greet her at the airport was Sir Winston Churchill and the first member of the Royal Family to acknowledge the new sovereign was her aged grandmother Queen Mary, who insisted on being the first to curtsy before her, as she had to her son Bertie and before him, to her eldest son David on the death of her husband King George V.

Queen Elizabeth II acceded to the throne on 6 February 1952, but was not crowned until 2 June 1953. The long delay between accession and coronation does not make any difference to the status or power of the sovereign. Indeed, from a constitutional point of view the coronation itself adds nothing. According to British law, the sovereign assumes the throne from the moment it is vacated: hence the ancient cry of 'The King is dead; long live the King.'

The long ordeal of the coronation ceremony and procession was followed by weeks of royal banquets, receptions and various other functions. London was full of dignitaries from all over the world, all anxious to pay their respects to the newly crowned Queen. The dawn of the second Elizabethan era saw the conquest of Everest by Edmund Hillary, knighted for his triumphant climb, and witnessed England's premier jockey Gordon Richards winning the Derby for the first time.

Queen Elizabeth II had become Queen not only of the United Kingdom, but of a large number of other countries, which today consists of: Australia; the Bahamas; Barbados; Canada; Fiji; Grenada; Jamaica; Mauritius; New Zealand; Papua New Guinea; Saint Lucia; St Vincent and the Grenadines; Solomon Islands and Tuvalu. She also became Head of the Commonwealth, including those countries with their own Head of State: at present Bangladesh; Botswana; Cyprus; Dominica; The Gambia; Ghana; Guyana; India; Kenya; Kiribati; Malawi; Malta; Nauru; Nigeria; Seychelles; Sierra Leone; Singapore; Sri Lanka; Tanzania; Trinidad and Tobago; Uganda; Vanuatu; Zambia and Zimbabwe; all of which are republics with a president as Head of State. Lesotho, Malaysia, Swaziland and Tonga have their own monarchies, while Western Samoa has a Paramount Chief as its elected Head of State.

The Commonwealth is a voluntary association made up of independent sovereign states which were formerly part of the British Empire. Most of the countries who belong to this 'family of nations' joined after the Second World War, when the break-up of the Empire really began, but the origins of the Commonwealth go back much further. It was in 1839 that Lord Durham published a report on the causes of discontent in the Canadian colonies. It was feared that if Britain did not agree to a certain amount of self-government, Canada might follow the example of their nearest neighbours in North America and secede from the British Empire. The British Government accepted Lord Durham's recommendations and from 1847 a system of 'responsible government' was in operation in Canada. Shortly afterwards it was extended to Australia, New Zealand and South Africa. This then was the beginning of what was to become the Commonwealth.

There is no compulsion for any of the former colonies to join the Commonwealth. It is an entirely voluntary organisation set up for the mutual benefit of its members. Countries can apply to join when they achieve independence – and they can leave whenever they choose. Eire left the Commonwealth in 1949 and became the Irish Republic and similarly, South Africa ceased to be a member in 1961 following criticisms of its racial policies at the Commonwealth Prime Ministers' Conference in March 1961. Also, a number of countries which were once the responsibility of Britain have decided not to join the Commonwealth: Burma, British Somaliland, Cameroon, the Republic of Maldives and Aden are among those who chose to remain outside the Commonwealth when they became independent.

In Britain, the Foreign and Commonwealth Office advises all other government departments on Commonwealth policy and provides information about its activities in Britain. All the member countries recognise The Queen as Head of the Commonwealth and because of this Commonwealth High Commissioners in London enjoy a special relationship with Her Majesty, dealing with her direct on all matters concerning their own country and the monarchy. In August 1973, President Julius Nyerere of Tanzania, speaking at the Commonwealth Heads of Government Meeting in Ottawa, said, 'The Commonwealth is not a matter of economics or technical co-operation. The Commonwealth is people meeting together, consulting, learning from each other, trying to persuade each other and sometimes co-operating with each other, regardless of economics or geography or ideology or religion or race. It is this which makes the Commonwealth valuable.' And President Kenneth Kaunda of Zambia, speaking in London in June 1977, said, 'Today we have an organisation not serving the British people and the British communities abroad but mankind as a whole. We are not members of this Commonwealth by accident of colonial history but by conviction.' In 1964, Prime Minister of New Zealand Sir Keith Holyoake described the Commonwealth as 'a great multi-racial association of nations'.

The main areas in which Commonwealth countries co-operate are: economic and social development, education, export market development, youth activities, applied studies in government and international affairs. Commonwealth members are able to make significant contributions to international efforts to solve world problems such as hunger, racial discrimination and health education. They do not normally discuss the internal affairs of a member country or take part in disputes between member states unless invited to do so. Government ministers hold frequent meetings with their opposite numbers, particularly those involved with finance, law, education and health. Large numbers of non-governmental organisations also maintain close contact within the Commonwealth.

In 1981, the Secretary-General Sir 'Sonny' Ramphal summed up the achievements and status of the Commonwealth in his report to the Heads of Government Meeting in Melbourne, Australia, when he said: 'It is not surprising that in many areas the Commonwealth has become a symbol of hope for consensus in a divided world.'

THE QUEEN'S FAMILY

The Duke of Edinburgh

His Royal Highness the Duke of Edinburgh was born on 10 June 1921 on the Greek island of Corfu. Until shortly before his marriage he was known as Prince Philip of Greece and at the time of his birth he was sixth in line of succession to the Greek throne. (One unusual fact about the circumstances of his arrival in the world is that he was born on the dining-table in his parents' villa, Mon Repos. Apparently the reason for this was simply that the attending doctor felt it would be better for the delivery than his mother's bed. It was certainly a unique entrance for a royal prince.)

Philip's parents were Prince and Princess Andrew of Greece, his father being a son of King George I of the Hellenes. He was educated in Scotland and fought in the Second World War as an officer in the Royal Navy. He had an unsettled childhood, mainly because his parents' marriage broke up while he was still very young and his father, like other members of the Greek royal family, was forced into exile. This resulted in Philip being shunted around between various European relations, until his uncle Dickie, Lord Mountbatten, took him under his wing and the Mountbatten family became his own.

The young Philip was among the first intake of pupils at the newly founded Gordonstoun School in 1934, where he excelled at games and other outdoor activities. Lord Mountbatten knew the founder of Gordonstoun, Kurt Hahn, and believed in the latter's theories of 'cold-water showers and plenty of outdoor activities'. By the time Philip left school he had become Head Boy, as well as captain of cricket and hockey. He was commissioned into the Royal Navy in 1940, serving on the battleship *Valiant* at the invasion of Crete.

In 1947 Prince Philip renounced his Greek title, assuming the surname of his uncle Lord Louis Mountbatten (and it was as Lieutenant Philip Mountbatten RN that his engagement to Princess Elizabeth was announced). This caused a great deal of discussion; a plebiscite in Greece had indicated that the monarchy was to be restored in that country and there was concern that if Philip gave up his title it would be seen as a slur. However, there was no legal reason why he should not be granted British citizenship; thousands of foreigners who had served in the armed forces were being naturalised every year, along with refugees from European countries which had been occupied by the Germans. One of the reasons why it was felt important for Philip to renounce his title and assume a new surname was that his original family name was Schleswig-Holstein-Sonderburg-Glucksburg. It was thought highly inappropriate for a British princess to marry someone with such an obviously German name so soon after the recent hostilities.

It was during the Royal Family's tour of South Africa that Philip became a British citizen. At the same time he also gave up his membership of the Greek Orthodox religion and was accepted into the Church of England. As he was about to marry the woman who would one day be Defender of the Faith it would have been impossible to have remained a member of another church, even though for all practical purposes he had considered himself to be an Anglican all his life anyway.

On the day before the royal wedding, King George VI announced that his future son-in-law had been created Duke of Edinburgh and would also be permitted to use the prefix 'His Royal Highness'. At the same time he was given the titles Earl of Merioneth and Baron Greenwich, but he was not created a Royal Prince until another ten years had passed, by which time of course his wife had become Queen. Philip is also a Knight of the Garter and a Knight of the Thistle; he is a Privy Councillor and he holds the Order of Merit. There is no official role or position within the British constitution for the husband of a Queen Regnant and the Duke has had to establish his own place in the nation's life. This he has managed to accomplish with great success, holding many important service appointments and acting as patron or president of a large number of national and international organisations. Unlike a number of his predecessors, he has refused to become 'just another royal figurehead' and every organisation with which he is involved feels his influence.

His Royal Highness has frequently aired his opinions on those issues he feels strongly about, and at the same time he manages to get things done through a genuine commitment to the task in hand. His main interests are the preservation of the environment, the welfare of the young – the famous Duke of Edinburgh Award Scheme has been running successfully for more than a quarter of a century – plus technology and science. His duties with many of the committees he chairs have seen him involved in a variety of topics from saving trees to new methods of spawning salmon. He also likes to try things out for himself: on a visit to Seattle in 1982 he took the controls of the newest Boeing 757 aircraft because, as a qualified pilot, he wanted to see how the aircraft handled. The Duke is an international horseman (see page 122), an accomplished sailor and an Admiral of the Royal Yacht Squadron. He has written a number of books, mainly on wildlife, on which he is an acknowledged authority, and those who know him best say he is prepared to go anywhere and meet anyone to argue for the causes he believes in.

The Duke of Edinburgh is known for his outspoken views on many diverse subjects. He has carried on a series of running battles with the Press for many years and one of the major criticisms voiced about him is that he is said to use his position to put forward his views knowing that very few people will disagree with him in public. The Queen keeps clear of controversy, the Duke seems to court it deliberately. Obviously he feels there are no constraints to be placed on him – he says what he feels, come what may. Now in his middle sixties he is still a lean, fit figure, even if arthritis makes him somewhat stiff and not quite as quick to move as he once was. His diary rarely has a vacant date and he has accompanied The Queen on every overseas State Visit since the accession. He may be required to take second place to The Queen on public occasions but it is as head of the family that he has really established himself. There is no doubt that he is the most powerful influence on Her Majesty and he has proved to be a stern but fair father to his four children. Every year they join him at Balmoral for a family get-together (without The Queen) when they review privately what has gone on in the past twelve months and discuss the prospects for the coming year. There are no absentees from this meeting and all four royal children know that if they have done something that Prince Philip disapproves of, they will hear about it in no uncertain terms.

He has fulfilled an active and important part in the public life of the nation, but as The Queen's husband his greatest success has been to provide a stable background for this most public of the world's families.

The Prince of Wales

The heir to the throne, Charles Philip Arthur George, was born in Buckingham Palace on 14 November 1948 and ten years later, at the closing ceremony of the Empire and Commonwealth Games in Cardiff, the recorded voice of The Queen announced that she intended to make her son Prince of Wales. His investiture took place at Caernarvon Castle on 1 July 1969, after Prince Charles had attended the University of Wales at Aberystwyth for a term to learn the basics of the Welsh language. His efforts to master one of the most difficult of tongues endeared him to the majority of the population and only the extreme Welsh nationalists were opposed to their new prince.

After service in the Royal Navy and the Royal Air Force, Prince Charles became a full-time Prince of Wales in 1976, when his service career ended. Like other members of the Royal Family he spends a great deal of his time working for charitable organisations, two of which he

21

instigated himself: The Prince's Trust and The Prince of Wales' Committee. These are not bodies to which he has merely lent his name. He is Chairman in every sense of the word, involving himself in the day-to-day activities and visiting their projects several times a year. He takes his responsibilities to the Principality of Wales very seriously and he has recently purchased a farm in Glamorgan in order to give himself a base in the country. This was bought through the Duchy of Cornwall, the traditional source of income for the Prince of Wales, and the Prince takes a practical interest in farming, even spending the occasional week working on the land himself. The Duchy is a large estate with vast agricultural holdings throughout the country and valuable properties in central London, including the Oval cricket ground. (Among the other titles held by The Queen's eldest son is the Dukedom of Rothesay, one of Scotland's most ancient, and whenever the Prince is in Scotland officially he is always referred to as the Duke of Rothesay.)

In recent years His Royal Highness has earned a reputation as being something of a 'progressive thinker' (or mild eccentric) mainly because of his attitude to alternative medicine, his care for the environment and the fact that since his marriage he has become more diet conscious. He eats red meat only once a week and has given up shooting at the urging of his wife. The Prince has definite views on modern architecture, describing a proposed addition to an important building in London's West End as a 'carbuncle' – which earned him a reprimand from the Royal Institute of British Architects and caused quite a stir in the Press. His unconventional views surprise many and shock a few, but that he is a caring, sincere and intelligent man can be in no doubt. Prince Charles has an insatiable appetite for finding out what is actually going on in the modern world, and if he does not entirely conform to the traditional notion of what a member of the Royal Family should be, is that necessarily a bad thing?

As an unofficial ambassador for Britain, Prince Charles has few equals. He is an enthusiastic traveller, either in his own right or on behalf of The Queen, and one of the most notable facts about his popularity is the way in which he is received in America, where he is welcomed in a manner which is quite remarkable in a land which has been a republic for more than 200 years.

On the morning of Tuesday 24 February 1981, the engagement was announced between the Prince of Wales and Lady Diana Spencer, daughter of the Earl Spencer, who was a former equerry to both The Queen and her father King George VI. The Queen interrupted an investiture at Buckingham Palace to tell her assembled guests who, after some encouragement from the Lord Chamberlain, broke with tradition by applauding the news. The wedding took place in St Paul's Cathedral on

29 July 1981, only the second royal wedding this century not to have been held in Westminster Abbey – the other was the wedding of the Duke and Duchess of Kent in York Minster. The reason St Paul's was preferred to Westminster Abbey was that 2500 guests could be accommodated in the Cathedral, with only 1800 in the Abbey.

Lady Diana Spencer was a teacher at a nursery school in London when she became romantically involved with Prince Charles. She was immediately followed everywhere by packs of reporters and cameramen capturing her every moment. She handled the Press brilliantly, even though she received no help from the Palace until the day the engagement was announced. 'Dianamania' grew to massive proportions in the long run-up to the wedding. Competitions were held to find Diana 'look-alikes'; her hair-style was copied by young girls all over the world and she had only to appear in a particular dress for it immediately to become the fashion of the moment. Reporters offered huge sums to her flat-mates to 'tell all' about the courtship and her lifestyle before the engagement – but none of them succumbed to the temptation. On the day of the wedding Diana appeared a true 'fairy-tale' princess in a stunning dress made by the Emanuels, designers David and Elizabeth, and a few weeks later the dress was sent around the country in a series of exhibitions so that people could see it in person. The wedding was the biggest media event ever seen. More than 500 million people watched it live on television in every country in the world and parties were held in streets up and down the country to celebrate. Ever since, millions of words in print are devoted to their lives each year, in particular to the Princess's clothes. The clothing industry has said publicly that she has done more for their business than any other single person this century and her choice of hats has led to a resurgence of the millinery trade.

While Prince Charles concerns himself with the business of running the Duchy of Cornwall and the other matters that demand his attention, the Princess has established her own routine of public duties. She has always genuinely cared a great deal about children and their welfare and this concern is shown in the causes she vigorously supports: Birthright and Deaf Children are just two.

The Prince and Princess occupy an apartment in Kensington Palace and their country home is Highgrove House in Gloucestershire, a few miles from Princess Anne's home and also that of Prince and Princess Michael of Kent. Highgrove is very much a family home: their first son, Prince William of Wales (William Arthur Philip Louis), was born on 21 June 1982 and their second, Prince Henry of Wales (Henry Charles Albert David), was born two years later on 15 September 1984.

Princess Anne

The Queen's only daughter, Her Royal Highness Princess Anne Elizabeth Alice Louise, Mrs Mark Phillips, GCVO (Dame Grand Cross of the Royal Victorian Order), was born in Clarence House on 15 August 1950. She has achieved a number of 'firsts' within the Royal Family: she was the first daughter of a sovereign to go away to school (Benenden in Kent); the first to win a major sporting title – when she became European Three-Day-Event Champion in September 1971 – and the first member of the Royal Family to be chosen to represent her country at an Olympic Games, which she did in Montreal in 1976.

The Princess combines a wide variety of roles in her private and public lives. Her two favourite charities are the Save the Children Fund, with which she has become totally identified since taking on the position of President in 1970, and Riding for the Disabled. She carries out more than 200 engagements a year and like all the other members of the Royal Family she has strong service connections. She is Colonel-in-Chief of four regiments, one of which, the 14th/20th King's Hussars, gave her a personal number plate for her car: it is 1420H – the regiment found it adorning an electric milk-float in West London!

Princess Anne was married to Captain Mark Phillips of 1st The Queen's Dragoon Guards, in Westminster Abbey on 14 November 1973 and since Captain Phillips left the army in 1976, the couple have lived at Gatcombe Park in Gloucestershire, on the estate bought for them by The Queen. They have two children, Peter Mark Andrew, born at St Mary's Hospital in London on 15 November 1977 and Zara Anne Elizabeth, born on 15 May 1981, neither of whom have titles although they are seventh and eighth in line of succession to the throne.

Mark Phillips is a working farmer looking after the 1500-acre (600-ha) estate that surrounds Gatcombe. He is also a successful competitor at international horse trials, taking part under the auspices of his sponsors the Range Rover Team. Awarded the CVO in 1974, following his efforts in preventing an attempt to kidnap Princess Anne, he is also a personal aide-de-camp to The Queen.

In December 1986, Princess Anne became head of the most important organisation in the equestrian world – the Federation Equestriane Internationale (FEI). The Princess was elected President in succession to her father, the Duke of Edinburgh, who was invited to become Honorary President. There were no votes against the Princess and the Duke said afterwards: 'Well, you've done better than I did!'

The FEI is involved in every aspect of equestrian sport, and Princess Anne, who is its youngest ever President, brings to it a personal knowledge of international competition in Three-Day Eventing and an extra dimension as a winning jockey on the Flat.

When she accepted the office, the Princess said she intends to be an active President and not just a figurehead. Speaking at the close of the FEI General Assembly, she said: 'There is so much scope within the disciplines for getting involved. . . . In international sport one must make sure that the sport survives the cross-fire of national interests.' With her practical experience as a horsewoman and her proven skills as a diplomat, Princess Anne could be just what the FEI needs.

Prince Andrew Duke of York

The Queen's second son Prince Andrew Albert Christian Edward was born at Buckingham Palace on 19 February 1960. Like his elder brother and father before him, he was educated at Gordonstoun in Scotland where he excelled at outdoor pursuits. He is also an accomplished linguist, speaking both German and French. After graduating from the Royal Naval College at Dartmouth he entered the Royal Navy on a twelve-year commission in 1980 and distinguished himself as a helicopter pilot during the Falklands Campaign in 1982. His ship HMS *Invincible* was involved in a number of attacks and Prince Andrew flying a Sea King helicopter came under enemy fire several times.

As a young man Prince Andrew was the royal who was always getting into scrapes. His early love-life gave the gossip columnists plenty to write about as he was frequently seen around London's fashionable nightspots with beautiful young women. He soon developed a playboy image and several of his girl-friends made sizeable sums from the newspapers by selling the stories of their romances with him. One or two invented sensational tales when the real thing wasn't hot enough for the papers. The one serious attachment he formed was with the actress Koo Stark – the only one never to utter a word about their relationship – but her background as an actress in soft porn films inevitably made her an unsuitable choice for marriage. His engagement to Miss Sarah Ferguson was announced on Wednesday 19 March 1986 and their wedding took place at Westminster Abbey on 23 July, just an hour after The Queen had created her second son the 14th Duke of York. Sarah Ferguson had also led an interesting life before she married. She had spent some years in Switzerland with a boy-friend many years older than herself and she had already established a successful career. Sarah is the daughter of Major Ronnie Ferguson, the Prince of Wales' polo manager, and she has known the Royal Family all her life, having played with both Prince Andrew and Prince Edward when they were all children. Prince Andrew intends to continue his naval career for the foreseeable future and the Duchess wants to do the same with her work.

Prince Edward

The youngest of The Queen's four children, Prince Edward Antony Richard Louis, was born in Buckingham Palace on 10 March 1964. His education followed that of his two older brothers, preparatory school and Gordonstoun, and he also spent a time in New Zealand teaching at a school in Wanganui. He graduated from Jesus College, Cambridge, with a degree in archaeology and anthropology and immediately joined the Royal Marines as a Commando Officer.

Physically, Edward is very different from either of his brothers. At six feet two inches (1.9m) he is the tallest member of the Royal Family and because of his height he sometimes looks slightly fragile, which is deceptive because he is in fact a tough, sturdy figure, as several of his opponents on the rugby fields of Cambridge found out. It was while he was at university that his other love – the theatre – became known. Edward was an enthusiastic member of the college drama society and he took part in a number of productions including one in which he danced and did acrobatics. When he was first accepted for entry into Jesus College there were protests from other students who claimed that he did not have the proper academic qualifications, but he silenced his critics after his three-year course by being awarded a 2.1 degree.

Prince Edward is considered to be one of the more sensitive of The Queen's children and he has not yet been subjected to the ordeal of trial by television as experienced by his brothers and sister. In fact he has let it be known that he does not care for the media at all and so far has given only two interviews to the Press. Now that his brother Andrew has been created Duke of York there is speculation about which title he may be given by The Queen when he marries. Suggestions have included the Dukedoms of Sussex and Connaught, but this is pure speculation at this time.

One of the ways in which he likes to relax is by helping with the harvest at Gatcombe Park, the home of his sister Princess Anne. He is a favourite uncle of both Peter and Zara Phillips and when they are all together at Balmoral during The Queen's summer break he frequently takes them on short excursions he devises to keep them amused. He is being introduced into the royal round of official duties very gradually and his most public appearance to date has been as supporter (best man) to Prince Andrew at his wedding. Prince Edward has a small suite of rooms at Buckingham Palace, which he shared with his elder brother Prince Andrew until the latter's marriage. Wing Commander Adam Wise is his Private Secretary and he has a lady clerk, but that is the extent of his staff at the present time.

The Queen Mother

Her Majesty Queen Elizabeth the Queen Mother was born Lady Elizabeth

Angela Marguerite Bowes-Lyon in London on 4 August 1900. She was the ninth of ten children of the Earl and Countess of Strathmore and the family seat was at Glamis Castle in Scotland. She married Prince Albert, 'Bertie', the second son of King George V, on 26 April 1923 and her husband acceded to the throne on the abdication of his elder brother King Edward VIII on 11 December 1936.

When her husband died on 6 February 1952, Queen Elizabeth moved from Buckingham Palace to Clarence House where she has lived ever since. She is associated with more than 300 organisations throughout the world and even at the age of eighty-six, she still carries out a large number of official engagements every year.

Her Majesty shares with her daughter The Queen a love of horse-racing and as an owner of steeplechasers, has had more than 350 winners. Her racing colours are blue with buff stripes and blue sleeves, and a black cap with a gold tassel.

Known affectionately throughout the world as 'the Queen Mum', no member of the Royal Family or the Royal Household would ever dream of calling her by that name. To the children of The Queen she is 'Granny' and to everyone else Queen Elizabeth; this distinguishes her from her daughter who shares her name and who is called simply 'The Queen'.

Princess Margaret

Her Royal Highness Princess Margaret Rose was born in Scotland at Glamis Castle on 21 August 1930. Her mother, then Duchess of York, wanted to name her Ann as she thought Ann of York would be a pretty title, but King George V indicated that he did not like the name and that was the end of the matter. King George VI had no such feelings and this was one of the reasons why, twenty years later, their own granddaughter was given the name Anne.

Since The Queen came to the throne in 1952, her sister has played an active part in the 'Royal Firm' and in 1954 she was the first member of the Royal Family to visit Germany after the war. It was at this time that she became romantically involved with Group Captain Peter Townsend who had been an equerry to her father, but eventually she announced that they would not marry (even though it would have been possible under Civil Law) because Group Captain Townsend was divorced. The Princess eventually married Antony Armstrong-Jones on 6 May 1960 at Westminster Abbey, the bridegroom being created Earl of Snowdon the following year.

Two children were born: David Albert Charles Armstrong-Jones, Viscount Linley, on 3 November 1961 and Lady Sarah Frances Elizabeth Armstrong-Jones on 1 May 1964. In May 1978, after eighteen years of marriage, Princess Margaret and her husband were divorced. He has since remarried but the Princess has never given the slightest indication of doing so. She still lives in the large apartment at 1a Clock Court, Kensington Palace, where she spent all her married life.

Since her divorce Princess Margaret has had her name romantically linked with a number of men, none of them from any of the remaining royal families in the world. She has chosen her friends mainly from the world of the arts. The late Peter Sellers was a particularly close friend until his death, and stars from the worlds of ballet and opera are often seen in her company. Perhaps the most widely publicised of her romances was with Roddy Llewellyn, the son of Col. Sir Harry Llewellyn, the former Olympic horseman. Roddy was eighteen years younger than the Princess and she was going through one of the bleakest moments of her marriage. Roddy was very similar in appearance to Lord Snowdon, apart from being an inch or two taller. He favoured blue jeans and sandals as his favourite form of dress and when he first met Princess Margaret he was wearing a silver stud earring in his left ear, which again must have appealed to her sense of the unconventional. He had an abundance of Welsh charm, which coupled with his fair good looks and soft voice made him a welcome addition to any dinner party. He and the Princess soon became inseparable, travelling to her holiday home on the island of Mustique with the small circle of friends who had served Princess Margaret for years. But the allegations that Llewellyn was responsible for the break-up of her marriage were wrong. Lord Snowdon and his wife had drifted apart long before Llewellyn came on the scene: he was just a convenient name for the Press to latch onto. After several years together Princess Margaret and Roddy Llewellyn broke up and he has since married, although they remain on friendly terms.

Her Royal Highness has suffered from ill health for some years, mainly because she refuses to give up smoking. Even after lung surgery in 1985 she returned to the habit, although she has cut down on the sixty cigarettes she used to smoke per day. She still likes to go to the theatre and most of her closest friends are involved in the arts in some way or other, but she also plays an important role carrying out royal duties as Patron of a number of organisations. Princess Margaret has close associations with the services; she is Colonel-in-Chief of a number of regiments and she keeps in touch with their activities constantly. Her civilian organisations include the Royal Ballet, of which she has been President since 1957, the Girl Guides Movement and St John Ambulance. In her younger days Princess Margaret was considered to be one of the most glamorous women in the world and she still has the most beautiful eyes, although her face these days reflects much of the sadness she has experienced in her life. She is an accomplished pianist, has a beautiful singing voice and a wicked talent for mimicry. And contrary to popular Press belief she remains on the closest terms with her sister and her mother.

These then are the immediate members of the Royal Family. There are of course many more on the fringes. When The Queen holds her traditional Christmas party at Windsor Castle nearly forty relations turn up, with the Gloucesters, the Kents and all their children: the cousins, nephews and nieces. The Royal Family today is a modern, working unit far removed from the cosseted and protected family of even fifty years ago. Queen Mary, the present Queen's grandmother, never used the telephone once in her entire life. She distrusted most modern inventions and did not believe they were meant to be. The Queen today could not possibly exist without the telephone. She calls her mother every day and speaks to Members of her Household constantly. If Princess Anne had been born a hundred years earlier she would never have been allowed to take part in horse trials or compete at international level in any sport whatever. Mark Phillips would certainly not have been considered suitable husband material for The Queen's only daughter and the thought of the heir to the throne marrying a commoner who came from a broken marriage would have caused a constitutional crisis. Princess Margaret's children go out to work and take no part in royal affairs. Even as recently as just before the Second World War this would have been unthinkable for the grand-children of the King, but today it would be just as unthinkable for them not to be gainfully employed. The Prince and Princess of Wales have been seen on television in the intimacy of their own home with their children wearing jeans and cowboy hats; whereas several generations ago they would only have been seen in public in formal dress and saying nothing. The Queen and her sister never went to school, they were educated privately, but The Queen's children all went away to school and her grandchildren even attend nursery school with other children of their own ages. The democratisation of the Royal Family has meant great changes in the last thirty years but there remains a strong dividing line between them and us. Democracy goes only so far and no further; the magic of monarchy has been maintained. While the rest of the family is seen as coming closer to ordinary people, The Queen herself remains above us all: she is the only one with any constitutional position. Everything revolves around her and whatever any other member of the Royal Family does, there is only one question that has to be answered – is it right for The Queen?

THE ROYAL HOUSEHOLD

One of the most exclusive organisations in the world goes under the collective title of the Royal Household. It refers to the men and women whose sole task is to ensure that the monarchy is run smoothly and efficiently. It is exclusive because those who belong to it have been invited to join – one cannot apply – and it maintains its air of exclusivity because its members never talk publicly about their jobs. There is a large number of former army officers in the Household, nearly all of them lieutenant-colonels from one of the more 'fashionable' regiments. A senior Member says the reason is that attention to detail is a prerequisite for all who would serve The Queen, so where better to search for men with such a quality than the Household Division.

There are three distinct levels within the Royal Household. At the top are the Members: Private Secretaries, Comptrollers and Assistants. In commercial terms these could be equated with managing directors, responsible for the day-to-day running of their departments. Then come the Officials, just below Assistant Private Secretary level, and they look after the administrative and clerical details. The third layer is referred to as Staff and they are the domestic (and clerical) employees, only a few of whom ever come into contact with members of the Royal Family.

There are a number of subtle but definite ways in which to tell which level of the Household one is dealing with. The Members all call each other by their Christian names, no matter how senior in years or service they may be. For example, the Crown Equerry, Lt.-Col. Sir John Miller, has been at Buckingham Palace for more than a quarter of a century but he is still called John by Vic Chapman, The Queen's Assistant Press Secretary, who ranks much lower in the scale and who has been in royal service for only a few years. Officials are called by their surnames, preceded by Mr, Mrs or Miss, and in turn they refer to Members by their titles; as many of the senior Members of the Household are knights, it is a convenient and simple rule to follow anyway. The Staff call everybody above them sir or madam. An ironic example of this is Miss Margaret McDonald, The Queen's dresser. 'Bobo', as she is affectionately known to Her Majesty, has been a close personal servant of The Queen for more than fifty years and she enjoys a unique position of considerable influence within the Royal Household. Nevertheless, in accordance with the correct procedure, she still calls Members of the Household, who are technically above her, 'sir' – even if she doesn't really mean it!

There are two Great Officers of State with titular responsibility in the Royal Household. The *Lord Great Chamberlain* was originally head of the sovereign's personal household and all royal palaces. The office dates back to the reign of King Henry I and has always been in the possession of three families: the Cholmondeley family (who are the present holders and who hold it every alternate reign) and the Ancaster and Carrington families, who each hold it every fourth reign. The family of the present Lord Carrington will take over on the death of The Queen. The present-day duties of the Lord Great Chamberlain consist of attending the coronation ceremony (where he stands on the left of the sovereign in Westminster Abbey, fastens the clasp of the Imperial Mantle after investiture, and arrays the sovereign in purple robes before the procession out of the Abbey) and making the arrangements when the sovereign attends the State Opening of Parliament.

The second Great Officer of State is the *Earl Marshal*, the Duke of Norfolk. The Earl Marshal is the premier Duke of England and the office originated in the reign of King Henry I. It has been hereditary in the Norfolk family since 1672. The Earl Marshal is head of the College of Arms and he has overall responsibility for the arrangements of the funeral of the monarch, other State funerals (for example the funeral of Sir Winston Churchill was a State funeral by order of The Queen) and the coronation. Apart from these duties he has little connection with the everyday running of the Royal Household.

Then there are the Great Officers of the Household: the Lord Steward, the Master of the Horse and the Lord Chamberlain. The duties remaining to the *Lord Steward* are few these days and are all purely ceremonial: attending the sovereign at a coronation; the State Opening of Parliament and the Lying-in-State of the previous dead monarch. The Lord Steward was originally responsible for paying all Household accounts and for making most of the domestic arrangements in the royal palaces. Again these latter responsibilities have passed to another official, the Master of the Household, but the Lord Steward retains his titular authority and is seen at State banquets walking backwards alongside the Lord Chamberlain as they precede the royal procession. The present Lord Steward is the Duke of Northumberland.

The *Master of the Horse* is presently the Earl of Westmorland. Once one of the most powerful positions at Court, the Master of the Horse still retains the right to ride immediately behind the sovereign on all ceremonial occasions. He is titular head of the Royal Mews but for all practical purposes the man responsible for running the stables and garages is the Crown Equerry. At one time, when the Royal Household also constituted the seat of government, the Great Officers of State were not only members of the sovereign's Household but officers of Parliament as well. However, as political democracy flourished in Britain, so the duties of the former Members of the Royal Household came to be assumed more and more by the political administration. Today we have the Lord Privy Seal; the Lord Chancellor; the Lord President of the Council; the Treasurer and the Comptroller of the Household; the Captains of both Royal Bodyguards; the Honourable Corps of Gentlemen at Arms; the Yeomen of the Guard and the Vice-Chamberlain of the Household, all as political appointments with governmental duties as well as their secondary responsibilities to the monarch.

The *Lord Chamberlain* is the Head of The Queen's Household. At present the post is held by the Earl of Airlie, elder brother of the Hon. Angus Ogilvy. The process by which Lord Chamberlains are appointed is known to only a select few. Lord Airlie's immediate predecessor was Lord Maclean, who until his appointment to the Royal Household had been Chief Scout of the Commonwealth for thirteen years. He says he returned from an overseas tour to find a message asking him to call Lord Cobbold, the then Lord Chamberlain, at St James's Palace. When he did so, Lord Cobbold told him quite bluntly that The Queen would like him to be her next Lord Chamberlain. There was no preamble and what is more there was no interview with Her Majesty. The first time Lord Maclean met his new employer as Lord Chamberlain, was on the day he became Head of her Household. To this day he still doesn't know how he got the job or who recommended him.

The Lord Chamberlain was originally a deputy to the Lord Great Chamberlain, but today he is completely independent. He is in charge of all ceremonial duties relating to the sovereign, apart from the funeral of the monarch, other State funerals and the coronation; these remain the responsibility of the Earl Marshal, the Duke of Norfolk.

The Lord Chamberlain has a wide variety of responsibilities as Head of The Queen's Household. He supervises all royal weddings; royal funerals; State Visits by overseas Heads of State; the Royal Garden Parties; the Chapels Royal and the cleaning of the Crown Jewels. He also looks after such disparate appointments as the Pages of Honour (the boys who attend the sovereign on State occasions); the Sergeants-at-Arms; the Marshal of the Diplomatic Corps; the Master of The Queen's Music; the Keeper of the Jewel House, Tower of London; the Poet Laureate; the Surveyors of Pictures and Works of Art; the Bargemaster and the Keeper of The Queen's Swans. In addition, the Lord Chamberlain acts as Her Majesty's emissary to the House of Lords.

Strange though it may seem, with so many varied responsibilities, there is no such thing as a job description for the Lord Chamberlain. Each incoming holder of the office is expected to make his own way and indeed this applies to many of the other important positions within the Royal Household. There are five departments in the Royal Household: the Private Secretary's Office; the Keeper of the Privy Purse; the Master of the Household; the Crown Equerry and the Lord Chamberlain's Office, though this last is something of a misnomer as the Lord Chamberlain himself has very little to do with the actual running of it. In fact the Lord Chamberlain does not have a department himself; he oversees all the others.

THE PRIVATE SECRETARY'S OFFICE

This is by far the most important department in the Royal Household. The Private Secretary is one of the most influential people in the country and is easily the most important person at Buckingham Palace, apart from The Queen herself. He is in day-to-day contact with Her Majesty, is responsible for her programme of events and is her link with Government. He sees every piece of correspondence that is addressed to The Queen and nobody, not even the Lord Chamberlain, manages to see her without his knowledge and consent. The present Private Secretary is an Australian who has been at Buckingham Palace since the early sixties. Sir William Heseltine was appointed to be The Queen's most confidential aide in April 1986 and he brought to the position a wealth of experience, having served in the Press Office and as both Assistant Private Secretary and Deputy Private Secretary, before his elevation to the highest post in the sovereign's personal office.

He accompanies The Queen on all overseas visits where his considerable diplomatic skills are combined with the complete discretion demanded of all The Queen's servants. The Private Secretary is also Keeper of The Queen's Archives, which are housed in the Round Tower at Windsor Castle, but much of the daily work on the archives (and it is considerable) devolves on the Assistant Deputy Keeper, who is also The Queen's Librarian. At present this post is occupied by Oliver Everett, who was formerly Assistant Private Secretary to the Prince of Wales.

The Press Office is another of the Private Secretary's responsibilities. The Queen's Press Secretary, Michael Shea, has an office just a few paces down the corridor from Sir William and no major decisions concerning the media coverage of the Royal Family are taken without his knowledge. There are two Assistant Press Secretaries, John Haslam, a former BBC radio producer, and Victor Chapman, a one-time professional football player in his native Canada, where he was also Press Secretary to the former Prime Minister, Pierre Trudeau.

The Queen's Flight is also the responsibility of the Private Secretary. Although there is a Captain of The Queen's Flight who runs the squadron on a daily basis, the ultimate responsibility for allocating aircraft rests with the Private Secretary's Office, and every request for permission to use the Flight comes to him.

It is impossible to overestimate the importance of the position of the Private Secretary in the Palace hierarchy. Although, in theory, all the department heads are equal in status, there is no doubt in anyone's mind where the real power lies. He is in frequent contact with the Secretary to the Cabinet and also with the Heads of State of all Commonwealth countries and he advises The Queen on all important matters of State. At the present time the Deputy Private Secretary is Robert Fellowes, a former stock-broker who is married to the elder sister of the Princess of Wales and whose late father was Land Agent to the Royal Estates at Sandringham. The Assistant Private Secretary is Kenneth Scott, who before being invited to join the Royal Household was British Ambassador to Yugoslavia.

KEEPER OF THE PRIVY PURSE AND TREASURER TO THE QUEEN

As the title implies, this office looks after the finances of the Royal Household, and the Keeper of the Privy Purse, Sir Peter Miles, is also Treasurer to the sovereign. As Keeper of the Privy Purse he looks after The Queen's private financial affairs: the Privy Purse; the Royal Estates; the Stud and Her Majesty's racing expenses. As Treasurer to The Queen he is also responsible for all Civil List finances. The original source of wealth for British monarchs was land. Succeeding sovereigns acquired great estates and valuable tracts of land (either through right of conquest or other more conventional means) until the peak of royal ownership, when it was said that in the mid-fifteenth century the monarchy owned more than one fifth of the total land area of the United Kingdom.

In 1760 King George III surrendered his income from nearly all the lands owned by the Crown in return for a fixed allowance from Parliament. This allowance was, and still is, known as the Civil List. The land that was surrendered by the King was administered by a Board of Commissioners appointed by the sovereign on the advice of the Prime Minister, and while the income from the land became the property of the Government, the property itself still belonged to the sovereign. That is still the situation today; the Crown Estate remains part of the hereditary possessions of the sovereign in right of the crown. It is not government property but neither is it part of the private estate of the reigning monarch.

There were two exceptions to the surrender of land by George III – the

34

Duchy of Lancaster and the Duchy of Cornwall. Both remained the private property of the sovereign. The income from the Duchy of Lancaster is still paid directly to The Queen and provides her annually with some £1·5 million. The estate consists of large areas of land in Lancashire, Yorkshire, Lincolnshire, Northamptonshire, Cheshire, Shropshire and Staffordshire, plus the most valuable single freehold of all – the ground on which stands the Savoy Hotel in the West End of London.

The income from the Duchy is used to fund the sovereign's private expenses via the Privy Purse. All the clothes in The Queen's wardrobe are paid for out of Duchy money; so too are Her Majesty's private donations to charity and the considerable sums spent on the upkeep of her homes at Sandringham and Balmoral, both of which are her private property and as such are not maintained by the State. Certain members of the Royal Family who carry out duties on behalf of The Queen but are not paid allowances through the Civil List are financed by the Duchy of Lancaster. The Duke of Gloucester, the Duke of Kent and Princess Alexandra all come into this category. The estates are managed by a council appointed by The Queen and the government keeps an eye on things through the office of the Chancellor of the Duchy of Lancaster, who is a junior Cabinet minister nominated by the Prime Minister with responsibility for approving the annual accounts. Her Majesty takes a close personal interest in the affairs of her Duchy, visiting some part of the estate at least once a year when, by ancient custom, she is toasted as 'The Queen, Duke of Lancaster'.

The other exemption to the Crown Estate is the Duchy of Cornwall, by tradition the source of revenue for the Prince of Wales since King Edward III created his son Edward, the Black Prince, the first Duke of Cornwall in 1337. Prince Charles is the 25th Duke of Cornwall and he has been in receipt of all the income from the Duchy since his twenty-first birthday in 1969. The Duchy is mainly an agricultural estate with vast holdings in Cornwall, Devon, Somerset, Dorset and Glamorgan but its most lucrative source of income is in fact its smallest; just forty-five acres (18 ha) in urban Kennington in south London, which includes some 600 houses and flats and The Oval, home of Surrey County Cricket Club. The Prince of Wales, as Duke of Cornwall, is also the owner of Dartmoor Prison and the surrounding moorland. The annual income from the Duchy of Cornwall is slightly in excess of £1 million. Since his marriage in 1981 Prince Charles has taken three-quarters and given the remainder to the Treasury in lieu of income tax. Neither he nor the Princess of Wales receive any money from the Civil List.

The Crown Estate is arguably Britain's biggest landlord, with agricultural land in England extending to 171,814 acres (69,531 ha). A further 95,717 acres (38,735 ha) in Scotland; 871 acres (352 ha) in Wales with another 67,000 acres (27,114 ha) of unenclosed waste of ancient manors, which are the subject of numerous common rights. There are slate quarries in North Wales; clay pits in Leicestershire; gravel pits in Yorkshire; tin mines in Cornwall; the rights to all gold and silver found on Crown land and it owns about half the foreshore around the coast of the United Kingdom. There are industrial estates at Ascot; Bingham; Cambridge; Devizes; Hemel Hempstead; Milton Keynes and Taunton. There are also office blocks from Plymouth to Doncaster and the Crown Estate owns the Royal Ascot Racecourse.

A large part of the income comes from the rents received on its commercial properties in central London. The Crown Estate owns shops and offices in prime positions in Oxford Street; New Oxford Street; Regent Street (including the former Swan & Edgar building at the corner of Piccadilly); The Haymarket (where its tenants include New Zealand House and the Theatre Royal); the whole of Trafalgar Square and property in the Strand. Many of the leading clubs in St James's south of Pall Mall pay rent to the Crown Estate and there are more offices and shops in Victoria and along Whitehall. There is a valuable site at Hyde Park Corner; residential property in Fulham and the magnificent Nash terraces surrounding Regent's Park. The Estate also has holdings all over outer London. In the financial year ending 31 March 1986, the rents from its London estates alone were £27,560,000, in addition to another £16 million from elsewhere in the United Kingdom, which meant that, after defraying management costs, the Crown Estate paid £26,500,000 into the Exchequer to be made part of the Consolidated Fund. The Consolidated Fund is the account from which the Civil List is paid to the sovereign each year to cover all working expenses.

Until The Queen came to the throne in 1952 the amount payable to the sovereign from the Civil List remained constant throughout the duration of the reign. This had been the case with every sovereign since King George III became the first monarch to receive an allowance from Parliament. The Queen's Civil List payment was fixed at £475,000 a year plus £95,000 a year to combat inflation. Within ten years, however, the figure was out of date. Another ten years passed before a Select Committee of the House of Commons recommended that the Civil List should be increased by more than 100 per cent. There was a detailed examination of all royal finances and a masterly report on the need for the increase was prepared by the then Lord Chamberlain Lord Cobbold, who was himself a former Governor of the Bank of England. The Civil List was increased to almost a million pounds and this sum remained the annual figure for just another three years before inflation once again demanded that the allowance should be reviewed. In 1975 Parliament decided that in future the Civil List would be increased every year, to keep in line with the rate of inflation.

The Civil List is not a salary for The Queen. Every penny is spent on expenses in running the Royal Household and other costs incurred in the course of The Queen's duties as Head of State. Neither is the Civil List the only source of finance with regard to the expenditure of the monarchy. Nearly three-quarters of all the costs arising from the official duties of the Royal Family is met by public departments – including the £3 million annual running costs of the Royal Yacht and the £5 million it takes to operate The Queen's Flight (both paid for by the Ministry of Defence); the £250,000 for the Royal Train (plus an extra £7 million in 1986 for the provision of new rolling stock); the upkeep of the royal palaces (the responsibility of the Department of the Environment) and State Visits overseas by members of the Royal Family for which the money is provided by the Foreign Office. All postal services for The Queen, members of her Family and the Royal Household are provided free of charge by the Post Office and telephone calls are paid for by the Department of the Environment.

The Queen pays no income tax on her allowance from the Civil List, but as nearly three-quarters of it goes on wages and salaries for staff and Members of the Royal Household, who are taxed in the normal way, most of it returns to the Exchequer anyway. Similarly the other members of the Royal Family who receive allowances under the Civil List pay no tax, but they are taxed on any other source of income. The income from the Duchy of Lancaster is also exempt from taxes and The Queen does not pay tax on her private wealth and income.

When the Civil List for 1985-6 was announced it was found that The Queen had been allocated an increase that was in fact less than the expected rate of inflation, so in real terms it was actually a pay-cut. Inflation was estimated to be around 5 per cent for the coming year and the Civil List increase was limited to 3·25 per cent.

The total breakdown of payments was:
The Queen £3,976,200
The Queen Mother £345,300
The Duke of Edinburgh £192,600
Princess Anne £120,000
Prince Andrew* £20,000
Prince Edward £20,000
Princess Margaret £116,800
Princess Alice, Duchess of Gloucester £47,300

37

The Duke of Gloucester   £94,000
The Duke of Kent   £127,000
Princess Alexandra   £120,900
Total   £5,180,100

* Prince Andrew (Duke of York) received an automatic increase on his marriage, making his allowance £50,000.

Of the total received, The Queen refunded £341,900 to the Treasury. This represents the amount paid to the Duke of Gloucester, the Duke of Kent and Princess Alexandra, whose working expenses are all paid by The Queen out of the Privy Purse.

There is also provision in the Civil List for an allowance of £60,000 a year to be paid to the widow of the Prince of Wales and in addition to the figures stated, another £310,000 was payable to the Royal Family from the Royal Trustees – the Prime Minister, the Chancellor of the Exchequer and the Keeper of the Privy Purse – in order to meet any approved increases in salaries and wages of staff working for the Royal Household.

The Privy Purse office controls all expenditure at royal residences including building, maintenance and decorating. When a new waiting room was needed at the Privy Purse Entrance to Buckingham Palace some years ago, it was the Master of the Household who decided it was needed, but it was the Keeper of the Privy Purse who had to find the money and authorise the work to go ahead.

The office looks after payments made from The Queen's private sources as well as official expenditure. For example, Her Majesty makes a large number of private donations to charities, either to large organisations or to individual cases which have been brought to her attention. There is never any publicity given to these gifts; that is usually one of the conditions laid down to the recipients. All these payments are made by the Treasurer's office who also look after the staff salaries and wages in the Royal Household. The Treasurer to The Queen works closely with her bankers, Coutts, and with her legal advisers, the old-established legal practice of Farrers. He is also Receiver-General of the Duchy of Lancaster and liaises with Lord Caernarvon, The Queen's Racing Manager, over the finances of Her Majesty's considerable investments in bloodstock.

Within the Keeper of the Privy Purse's department there is also an ancient-sounding sub-department known as the Royal Almonry. It is headed by the Lord High Almoner, the Lord Bishop of Rochester, and in centuries past the office was responsible for distributing alms to the poor on behalf of the sovereign. These days its sole task is to look after the administrative details of the annual Maundy Service when The Queen gives a bag full of coins, one for each year of her life, to the same number of men and women.

THE MASTER OF THE HOUSEHOLD

There are more than 200 domestic staff employed at Buckingham Palace and each one comes under the jurisdiction of the Master of the Household. The present holder of this position is Rear Admiral Sir Paul Greening, who was formerly Flag Officer Royal Yachts. He retains an interest in his former command because the Master of the Household is responsible for the provisions on board *Britannia* whenever a member of the Royal Family is embarked.

The job of controlling the various domestic departments within the Household is a particularly demanding one. There are more than eighty functions held every year in Buckingham Palace alone, ranging from the small informal luncheons given by The Queen for a dozen guests to the three annual Garden Parties to each of which some 9000 guests are invited. The catering for these large events is left to J. Lyons Ltd who have wide experience in feeding large numbers, but the overall responsibility for the standard of the food and drink is still the Master of the Household's.

Every day more than 600 meals are served at the Palace. The senior Members of the Household help themselves at breakfast and lunch in a decidedly informal manner. There is no particular seating arranngement apart from one place reserved for the Master of the Household, who has a small silver bell by his side, a relic from the days when he would ring for the next course to be served. Everyone else can sit wherever they choose and this is an extremely useful way for various Members to meet their colleagues and exchange information. For example, in the normal course of the day few people come into contact with the Lord Chamberlain outside his own department. At mealtimes anyone can come up and sit next to him if they want to have a few words. For a short period Members were charged for their meals, but the administrative costs of collecting the money were higher than the amount charged, so the practice was discontinued and all the meals are now free.

The Officials have their own dining room in another part of the Palace and the domestic staff eat in a cafeteria. Of the entire complement of more than 200 people employed at the Palace, less than a dozen come into regular contact with the Royal Family. The majority is employed in looking after the people who work for The Queen. There is even one man whose tasks include winding the 300 clocks the Palace contains. According to Lord Maclean, the former Lord Chamberlain, Her Majesty takes a keen interest in all domestic arrangements and the Master of the Household confers with her every Monday to finalise the menus for the coming week. When visitors are expected, The Queen will personally inspect the rooms beforehand to make sure everything is in order and with two or three State Visits every year, either at Buckingham Palace or Windsor, individual tastes and preferences are an important part of the Master of the Household's job.

Among the staff at Buckingham Palace is a number of servants whose titles originated in medieval times but whose duties today are as vital to the smooth running of the monarch's domestic life as ever.

Palace Steward He is the head servant in the Royal Household with responsibility for all male servants including the Pages of the Presence, the Page of the Chambers, the Pages of the Backstairs, the Sergeant Footman and all the Footmen, the Yeomen of the Gold and Silver Pantry, of the China and Glass Pantry and of the Royal Cellars. He also looks after the serving arrangements at all State Banquets, lunches and dinners given by The Queen.

Page of the Chambers He looks after the serving arrangements at cocktail parties and other occasions and he is on duty at The Queen's engagements within the Palace, such as Investitures and the presentation by foreign ambassadors of their Letters of Credence.

Pages of the Presence These are the servants who come into most contact with the outside world. They are in charge of the Privy Purse Door where visitors to the Household are received; they also look after the Grand Entrance and the entry and departure of all ambassadors and others being received in audience by The Queen. When visiting members of Royal Families stay at Buckingham Palace or Windsor Castle, the Pages of the Presence act as personal servants if required. One daily task they have is to see that Members of the Household always have fresh stationery on their desks.

Travelling Yeoman This indispensable servant is responsible for the luggage arrangements for The Queen and those members of the Household when they are travelling. As his title suggests he travels with The Queen to all the royal residences including the Royal Yacht, on board the Royal Train and overseas.

Yeoman of the Gold and Silver Pantry The Queen's collection of gold and silver, plate, candelabra, cups and ornaments is arguably one of the finest in the world and this man is responsible for keeping an inventory and making sure each piece is in perfect condition. Whenever there is a State Banquet the Yeoman of the Gold and Silver Pantry looks after the displays of gold plate – and then makes sure every piece is accounted for afterwards.

Yeoman of the Glass and China Pantry Equally valuable is The Queen's collection of china and glassware and this man has overall responsibility for it. With more than eighty functions a year held in Buckingham Palace alone, apart from all the other meals served, his is a massive task.

Yeoman of the Royal Cellars The cellars at Buckingham Palace and all the other royal residences are vast and well stocked with a variety of vintage wines, malt whiskies, beers and soft drinks. The Yeoman of the Royal Cellars looks after them all.

The Queen's Pages There are two Pages of the Backstairs, both of whom are very senior male servants who have been in royal service for many years. They take it in turn to wait in attendance on Her Majesty, so there is always one on duty. If a Member of the Household wants to see The Queen he speaks first of all to the Page to find out if The Queen is free. This is a position very close to The Queen and her Pages are required to be models of discretion.

The Flagman This man is a serving soldier from the Household Division who has been recommended by his Commanding Officer and selected by the Master of the Household. Apart from running the Royal Standard up when The Queen is in residence (and down when she is not) he also sends off flags whenever they are needed for a visit by Her Majesty, and sees that they are returned safely afterwards. Because security is now of such prime importance, the Flagman also acts as the principal operator in a team of three which scrutinises by fluoroscope every parcel and item of mail arriving through the post at Buckingham Palace.

Domestic staff at Buckingham Palace are members of the Civil Service Union and their pay is negotiated on a scale analogous to the Civil Service, but the Union, recognising the unique and delicate position of its members within the Royal Household, normally excludes royal employees from industrial action. They have not yet had a strike at Buckingham Palace!

THE CROWN EQUERRY

Efficiency is taken for granted in all the departments surrounding the monarchy. Everything runs on time and according to the planned programme. The Queen and her family never seem to hurry and yet they always arrive in exactly the right place at exactly the right moment. Obviously it is no accident. Every minute of every day is meticulously planned many months in advance and the business of getting the Royal Family through rush-hour traffic, in hail, rain or snow, is all part of the everyday routine for the man who runs the Royal Mews.

The Crown Equerry is Deputy to the Master of the Horse and he organises all transport for The Queen, whether it is to be by private motor car, official limousine, State carriage or on horseback.

Lieutenant-Colonel Sir John Miller, KCVO, DSO, MC, is a former Commanding Officer of the Welsh Guards and he has been at Buckingham Palace for more than a quarter of a century. He is one of Her Majesty's most trusted servants and has become a personal friend of all the Royal Family. It was Sir John who first introduced Princess Anne to the sport of Three-Day Eventing and the Duke of Edinburgh to Four-in-Hand Carriage Driving. He has been responsible for teaching all the younger members of the Royal Family to ride and he is regarded as one of the world's foremost authorities on equestrian matters.

Sir John's attention to detail is legendary in Palace circles and when he is dealing with the unpredictable behaviour of teams of horses pulling coaches weighing four tons (4.064 tonnes) he leaves nothing to chance. In 1969 at the Investiture of the Prince of Wales at Caernarvon Castle, he went over the route of the royal procession no fewer than seven times, each time with stop-watch in hand, checking and rechecking the different elements which could possibly affect the timings on the day. At one point there was a steep incline around the Castle wall. Sir John rode in the coach that would carry the Prince of Wales and instructed his assistants to throw buckets of water in front of the horses' hooves so that he could see how rain might affect their performance. Then he had the banners which would be hanging outside the Castle walls shaken vigorously so that if a gale was blowing on the day of the Investiture, he could see if they would disturb the horses. Nothing escaped his trained eye – and as usual the programme went like clockwork.

The Royal Mews gives the impression that little has changed in the 200 years it has been located in the south-west corner of Buckingham Palace, and indeed, physically it does look much the same. It was in 1824, four years after George IV acceded to the throne, that the architect John Nash was asked to redesign the stables and coach houses at Buckingham Palace. The work took a year to complete and in 1825 the Royal Mews came into being. The date can still be seen on the weathercock above the entrance porch. Of course, Nash's original design was intended just for horses and State Carriages; the horses are kept on the west and north wings, with the State Coaches in their original home in the east wing. The twentieth century has intervened with the inclusion of the motor cars and royal limousines which are garaged in former coach houses behind the quadrangle, which have been converted for the purpose.

I remember one occasion when I had been invited to stay for lunch with Sir John at his elegant house just inside the Mews Gate. Before we sat down he showed me around. In the basement, where the kitchens were located in the last century, there was a massive cooking range which was so big it would be impossible to remove it – and these days it would be so expensive to run that no one could afford it. There are rooms especially allocated for the cleaning of riding boots, others for whips, the storing of various items of equipment and yet more for the different outfits worn by the Crown Equerry in days long gone. Sir John told me that in Queen Victoria's reign, the Crown Equerry had a personal domestic staff of ten to look after him and his family – all provided by the sovereign free of charge. Today, Sir John, who is a bachelor and lives alone, manages with the help of a single housekeeper and an occasional part-time helper. There are thirty horses quartered in the Mews and if they live in what seems to be extremely luxurious stables, there is a very practical reason. They all have to earn their keep; they are in constant use, and by keeping them in warm, dry, comfortable stalls, the Crown Equerry is able to get longer and more efficient use out of them. The horses are not, for instance, kept solely for State occasions. They are in daily use pulling the carriages that are used to collect foreign ambassadors and bring them to the Palace to present their credentials. They convey the Yeomen of the Guard to their places of duty and collect and deliver certain documents from one royal residence to another.

The Crown Equerry also provides cars for the Royal Family for every occasion. The five State Rolls-Royces are kept in immaculate condition and none of them has ever been through an automatic car wash. Each one is carefully hand-washed, dried and polished and kept in a heated garage when not in use. Just as carefully serviced are the lawn mowers and hedge cutters, which also come under the umbrella of the Crown Equerry's department, together with some dozen or so chauffeurs, forty-odd grooms and coachmen and ninety maintenance men and women. The latter includes the seamstresses who sew the exquisite uniforms worn on State occasions and the upholsterers who look after the padding in the coaches and carriages.

The Crown Equerry is known to prefer horses to machines, a preference he is delighted to acknowledge, especially on the rare occasions when one of the royal cars breaks down. As he says: 'It's never been known to happen with a horse.'

THE LORD CHAMBERLAIN'S OFFICE

The department which bears the name of the Head of the Royal Household is not in fact headed by the Lord Chamberlain himself, but by the Comptroller of the Lord Chamberlain's Office – at present Lt.-Col. Sir John Johnston, KCVO, MC. The office is located in St James's Palace in what used to be the home of the late Duke of Gloucester. Here it is responsible for all the ceremonial surrounding the monarchy. When The Queen goes to the Palace of Westminster for the State Opening of Parliament, it is the Comptroller, accompanied by the Assistant Comptroller and the Gentleman Usher to the Sword of State, who journeys to the Palace of Westminster with the Imperial State Crown which Her Majesty wears on these occasions. When the Duke and Duchess of York were married in Westminster Abbey on 23 July 1986 it was the Comptroller and his small staff who organised the ceremonial and the guest list. And when the late Duchess of Windsor was buried beside her husband in the Royal Vault at Frogmore in Windsor Great Park, it was the Lord Chamberlain's Office which took care of all the arrangements, including coordination with Kenyon's, the firm of undertakers which has had responsibility for all royal funerals for generations.

Among the many responsibilities of the Lord Chamberlain's Office is the administration of the Royal Warrants. If an individual or company has been supplying goods or services to a member of the Royal Family for three years, he, she or they are entitled to apply for a Royal Warrant. This would enable them to display a handsome coat of arms on their letter headings and over the doorway of their premises, together with the legend saying that the holder is a supplier to a particular member of the Royal Family. These warrants are highly sought after and are allocated only after a rigorous investigation by the Lord Chamberlain's Office.

All would-be recipients of honours in the Royal Victorian Order, the sovereign's personal order of chivalry, come under the scrutiny of the Lord Chamberlain. He is Chancellor of the Order and deals with all promotions, even though the heads of the individual departments within the Royal Household normally suggest the names of those people who they feel should be considered.

Perhaps one of the most intriguing departments within the Lord Chamberlain's Office is the Garden Party Office. This is staffed by a number of ladies who in early summer write out in longhand some 31,000 invitations every year. These ladies still go by the old-fashioned title of 'Temporary Lady Clerks', even though some of the 'Temps' have been doing the job for many years. Every name is filed and indexed and a great deal of attention is paid to titles, decorations and professional qualifications on the invitations.

In another part of St James's Palace is the office of the Surveyor of The Queen's Pictures. Sir Oliver Millar has been in royal service for forty years and has become one of the world's foremost authorities in his field. He is responsible for more than 5000 paintings in the Royal Collection which are spread throughout all the royal residences including Balmoral,

Sandringham and the Palace of Holyroodhouse in Edinburgh. When fire destroyed a large part of Hampton Court Palace in March 1986, Sir Oliver was one of the first on the scene to assess the damage to the priceless paintings hanging in the Palace. He has a small restoration studio in St James's Palace and there he is able to restore many paintings in the Royal Collection.

An equally important position within the Royal Household is that of Surveyor of The Queen's Works of Art. Sir Geoffrey de Bellaigue occupies this post which gives him the awesome responsibility of looking after all works of art in the Royal Collection other than paintings. There is a very nice tradition in the Royal Household by which Members are allowed by The Queen to borrow paintings from her collection to hang in their own rooms if they do not have any pictures of their own. So you might have the Press Secretary with a valuable Canaletto or Rubens to look at for a few months or Princess Anne's Private Secretary choosing a Lowry. The pictures are usually changed around every six months or so. There are so many small departments within the Household, such as the Central Chancery of the Orders of Knighthood, the Honourable Corps of Gentlemen at Arms and The Queen's Bodyguard of the Yeomen of the Guard, that it would be impossible to list them all, but each one comes under one of the five main departmental heads: the Private Secretary; the Comptroller of the Lord Chamberlain's Office; the Keeper of the Privy Purse; the Master of the Household or the Crown Equerry.

Apart from The Queen herself, other members of the Royal Family have their own Households. The Prince and Princess of Wales employ a Private Secretary and a Treasurer, an Assistant Private Secretary, a Comptroller and two Equerries. The Duke of Edinburgh has his own private office at Buckingham Palace (said to be the most automated office in the Palace), while Princess Anne, the Duke and Duchess of York, Prince Edward, Princess Margaret, Princess Alice, the Duke and Duchess of Gloucester and the Duke and Duchess of Kent all have their own Private Secretaries and Household staff. There is only one female Private Secretary and that is Miss Mona Mitchell, Private Secretary to Princess Alexandra, whose tiny office in Friary Court, St James's Palace, is one of the friendliest and most efficient in the entire Household.

One department which is not strictly within the Royal Household but is nonetheless a vital part of its everyday existence, is the Royal Protection Squad. This is provided by the Metropolitan Police at New Scotland Yard and is under the personal supervison of a Deputy Assistant Commissioner. Every member of the Royal Family is assigned a personal detective, and most have three who work around the clock. At the top is Detective Chief Superintendent James Beaton who is The Queen's personal police officer. He accompanies Her Majesty on all visits overseas and he (or one of his colleagues) is the person who sits alongside the chauffeur in the royal limousine.

Mr Beaton first went to Buckingham Palace as Princess Anne's detective and he was involved in the dramatic kidnap attempt in The Mall in March 1974, when a gunman tried to abduct the Princess as she returned to Buckingham Palace from an engagement with her husband. Four people were shot including the then Inspector Beaton who was wounded three times. The Princess and Captain Mark Phillips had been married less than five months when the incident happened. It was shortly after 7.30 p.m. when the royal car, an Austin Princess limousine, was passing St James's Palace just a few yards short of Buckingham Palace, when it was forced to stop by a Ford Escort. A man leapt out of the car and fired a gun at the limousine, hitting Inspector Beaton in the chest. The assailant managed to open the rear door on Princess Anne's side and grabbed her by the arm, pulling her towards him. Mark Phillips grabbed her other arm and a tug-of-war ensued which Mark won, pulling his wife (who was unharmed) back into the car. Her Lady-in-Waiting Rowena Brassey had meanwhile opened the door on her side of the car and crawled out where she lay crouched in the gutter. The attacker shot Inspector Beaton twice more, in the hand and through the stomach. The Princess spoke to the gunman, asking him what he wanted. He replied, 'I'll get a couple of million.' Eventually police reinforcements arrived but not before the chauffeur, Reg Callender, a passing civilian who tried to help and another police constable had been shot. The man was finally overpowered and the Princess and her husband continued their journey to Buckingham Palace. In court the attacker was identified as Ian Ball, whose plan had been to kidnap the Princess and hold her for a ransom of £3 million to be paid in £5 notes. He had made detailed plans of where he intended to keep her prisoner and his ransom note, which was addressed to The Queen, demanded a free pardon for himself of all offences 'from parking to murder'. Ball was ordered to be detained in a special hospital under the Mental Health Act without limit of time. All the people, police and civilians, who helped protect Princess Anne received awards from The Queen for their bravery, with Inspector Beaton receiving the George Cross, the highest honour for valour awarded to civilians.

The Royal Protection Squad is made up of volunteer police officers from all over the country. They go through a rigorous selection procedure before being allocated to one of the Family. Each one is an expert at unarmed combat but also carries a gun. From time to time they go on refresher courses at the Special Air Services Headquarters in Hereford, to keep them fully up to date with the latest developments in security precautions.

Being a member of the Royal Protection Squad becomes a way of life and the Royal Family is very aware of the disruptive effect on family life this can mean. So the wives and children of members of the Squad are often included in invitations to Garden Parties and other appropriate occasions, so that the Royal Family's appreciation can be shown in a very positive way.

So this is the Royal Household; an amalgam of some 300 people of varying backgrounds and talents, each one dedicated to the service of the sovereign and each one in his or her own way an essential part of the whole. The Lord Chamberlain at the top, for instance, says he knows how important it is for the most junior footmen to realise they are as much a part of the team as he is himself.

There are a few perks for those working at Buckingham Palace. Many of the Staff and Officials, for instance, live in comfortable 'Grace and Favour' homes provided rent free by a grateful employer and continue to do so long after they have retired. And being part of the Royal Household is like living in a village, with its own community, gossip, rumours and hierarchy. Many of its members come from families with generations of service to the Crown; some on the domestic side have been recruited straight from the job centre. Nobody gets rich serving The Queen but many of those who work for her say that nothing else gives the same satisfaction of knowing that, by doing their job properly, they are making life that much easier for Her Majesty – who, they insist, works harder than any of them!

ROYAL HOMES

Buckingham Palace, London SW1, is an address that is known all over the world. Ask any tourist from Tokyo to Tennessee what they would most like to see on a visit to Britain's capital and the answer will invariably be 'Buckingham Palace'. And yet, even though this is where The Queen spends most of her working year, and is to all intents the home of the sovereign, it is really only the principal official residence of the monarch.

Her Majesty herself regards Windsor Castle, twenty miles (32km) to the west, as being very much more a home. She spends every weekend there and favoured guests are invited to stay with her in the Private Apartments. Almost all official guests are accommodated at Buckingham Palace. The royal residences can be divided into those which are owned and maintained by the State and those which are the private property of The Queen, for whose upkeep she is responsible from her personal income. The royal palaces Buckingham Palace, Kensington Palace, Hampton Court Palace, Windsor Castle (still a royal palace, even though it was built as a fortress), the Palace of Westminster (which retains its royal status as the seat of government), and, in Scotland, the Palace of Holyroodhouse, are all owned and maintained by the State and are used by the sovereign only during his or her reign. They are then handed on to the succeeding monarch.

The private homes of The Queen are Balmoral in Scotland and Sandringham House in Norfolk. Both of these were left to her by her late father King George VI, who in turn had inherited them when they were handed over by Edward VIII on his abdication. The cost of maintaining these two homes is borne by The Queen, apart from security, which remains the responsibility of the State wherever she is staying.

BUCKINGHAM PALACE

This great mansion at the end of The Mall was built by John Sheffield, Duke of Buckingham, and completed in 1708. Even in those days it was regarded as the finest site in London and the King, George II, wanted to buy it as soon as he saw it. But the Duke of Buckingham's widow, who was living in far greater style than her royal neighbours in St James's Palace, refused to part with Buckingham House, as it was then known. Eventually it was sold to King George III in 1762 and on 22 May of the same year His Majesty and his 18-year-old consort, Queen Charlotte, moved into the house – the first royal couple to occupy it.

The mansion became known as the Queen's House from that date on and all but one of Queen Charlotte's fifteen children were born there, the only exception being her first son, the Prince of Wales, later George IV. In fact it was George IV who was responsible for the appearance of the Palace as we know it today. When he acceded to the throne he commissioned the architect John Nash to design him 'a palace fit for a king'. In due course this was achieved, but George IV died before the work could be completed and Queen Victoria was to be the first sovereign to make Buckingham Palace her official home when she moved there shortly after her accession in 1837.

Thirteen years later, the marble arch which dominated the east front was removed to its present location on the north-east corner of Hyde Park. The arch was completely out of proportion with the remainder of the Palace and, magnificent though it was, its position obscured the view down The Mall and prevented the crowds that even then gathered in front of the Palace railings from seeing clearly into the forecourt.

Visitors to the Palace today enter by the North Centre Gate – which is the one on the extreme right as you look at Buckingham Palace from The Mall. There are always at least two police officers on duty and if you are expected, you will be directed across the forecourt towards the Privy Purse Door. Until 1982, it was possible for anyone to enter Buckingham Palace, simply by asking to sign The Queen's Visitors' Book. To do this you would be led into a small reception room just to the right of the entrance, where the book was laid on a table ready for your signature. It only took a few moments and every year thousands of tourists took this opportunity, so that they could say that they had been inside Buckingham Palace. It was a pleasant and harmless custom and it is a sad reflection of our times that because of the ever-present threat of terrorists, the practice was discontinued.

For the expected visitor, a rather unusual feeling is experienced as you walk the fifty yards (45m) across the loose gravel of the forecourt to the Privy Purse Door. Millions of people have pressed their faces up against the railings around the Palace wondering what it's like inside; now for the first time you have an entirely different perspective as you look back at all the faces looking in at you. They seem to be wondering who you are and what your business is at Buckingham Palace – it's a strange but not altogether unpleasant sensation.

Inside the Palace you are asked to wait in a small room just off the hall. It is furnished with gilt chairs covered with lime green silk and there are two writing tables (with no notepaper since visitors began taking the headed sheets as souvenirs). You will be offered two newspapers to read: *The Times* and the *Daily Express*. No one seems to know why these two papers are preferred at Buckingham Palace but they are the only two I have ever seen in the waiting room. There are three large paintings on the walls. On my last visit they were: *Departure Scene at Paddington Station* by W. P. Frith; *Inspection of the Troops at Madrid* by King Edward VII, and a charming French water-colour of a provincial town. After just a few minutes – punctuality is a byword in Palace circles – you will be conducted by a liveried footman along the silent, red-carpeted corridors to the person you have come to see. All the offices of those closest to The Queen, her Private Secretaries and Press Secretaries, are situated off the ground-floor corridor along the north side of the Palace, overlooking the side gardens and immediately below the apartments of The Queen. None of the rooms of the Private Secretaries are luxurious in the modern sense of the word, but they are furnished in the most comfortable style with large, antique desks and deep leather armchairs. By long-standing tradition the doors of all the rooms are open and occasionally you pick up fascinating snippets of conversation as you pass by, with phrases like 'I think The Queen would like that . . .' or 'Her Majesty cannot make it on that day I'm afraid.'

If you happen to be visiting around 4.30 p.m. you may be lucky enough to be invited to take tea in the Equerries' Withdrawing Room. All the senior Members of the Household who are in the Palace gather to drink India or China tea out of cups decorated with the royal cypher and eat tiny sandwiches and light, fluffy cakes. They only stay for a few minutes but it's a pleasant break in a working day which, for many in the Royal Household, can last until well into the late evening.

The Queen's apartments are on the first floor of the north side over-looking Green Park. They are very easy to recognise from the road outside because only one room has a bow window. She enters and leaves the Palace by the Garden Entrance, which is also on the north side and which opens on to Constitution Hill, so the crowds of tourists who hang around the main entrances to the Palace will only rarely see her leaving or arriving. One of the homely touches in the part of the Palace occupied by The Queen is the number of toys which can sometimes be seen left in the corridors, waiting for the next visit by one of her grandchildren. The Queen has a private lift to her apartments and those of her husband and this is used only by members of the Royal Family. The only room in the Private Apartments which is regularly seen by outsiders is The Queen's Audience Chamber, where she receives diplomatic guests who are in London on official business, or occasionally somebody on a personal basis, such as the widow of a man who has been posthumously decorated for gallantry. It is also the room in which The Queen receives the Prime Minister on Tuesday evenings for the weekly audience, when they talk alone together about affairs of state. It is a light, elegant and airy room whose walls are decorated in a pale shade of green. The chairs and sofa are upholstered in fawn silk and there is a profusion of small tables laden with royal photographs.

The ground floor of Buckingham Palace is the working area where most of the offices are located, although there is also some office accommodation on the second floor. Princess Anne has a small suite of rooms on the second floor, immediately above the central balcony, and her offices – three rooms for Private Secretary, Personal Secretary and Clerk – are right next door, in what used to be the Palace schoolroom. Also on the second floor, in the extreme left-hand corner as you look at the Palace from the front, is the Ladies-in-Waiting Sitting Room. This is a delightful, light, airy room furnished in country-house style with chintz-covered chairs and sofas.

The main or principal floor of the Palace is the first floor. This is where all the State Rooms are located, which are reached via the Grand Staircase, a magnificent construction of Carrara marble designed by Nash, with gilt bronze balustrading by Samuel Parker. One of the main State Rooms is the Throne Room, the setting for the wedding group photograph of the Duke and Duchess of York in July 1986, whose most striking feature is the dazzling beauty of the seven cut-glass chandeliers, adapted for electric light in 1901. Others include: the Ballroom, more than 100 feet (30m) long and 60 feet (18m) wide and used for the fourteen investitures which take place every year (when families of the recipients of the honours are permitted to witness the ceremony); the State Dining Room, dominated by a massive portrait of George IV in coronation robes overlooking the huge mahogany table which can seat sixty guests; the Music Room, with its eighteen columns of deep blue scagliola where all royal christenings at Buckingham Palace take place (the chapel was destroyed by bombs during the Second World War); and the White Drawing Room, which is entered from the Royal Closet through a concealed door with swinging mirror and table. Here the Royal Family assembles on State occasions before processing to the Ballroom, and to the room which has been described as the most beautiful in the Palace, the Blue Drawing Room. Large and elegant, this was frequently used as a ballroom before the present one was built. Situated between the Music Room and the State Dining Room, the Blue Drawing Room is a lofty apartment whose richly carved ceiling is supported by columns of Carrara marble. There are four magnificent crystal chandeliers and the heavy silk curtains and gilt chairs are all in a cool shade of ice blue, in keeping with the general theme of the room. The Blue Drawing Room is dominated by a massive Chinese carpet whose main colour is red, but the blue from which the room gets its name is woven into the intricate pattern. Visitors who see the Blue Drawing Room for the first time are usually unanimous in acclaiming its beauty and there are few rooms in the Palace to rival its elegance, style and grace.

The most exotic room in the Palace is the Chinese Luncheon Room, where The Queen and the Duke of Edinburgh sometimes entertain guests at the small, informal lunches they hold about a dozen times a year. The furnishings and fabrics were taken from George IV's Banqueting and Music Rooms at Brighton Pavilion and always provide a topic of conversation for those seeing them for the first time. The walls are blue and covered with Chinese paintings; the curtains are crimson; the dining chairs light pink and the carpet turquoise. There is an enormous gilt mirror over the marble fireplace which reflects the pieces of Chinese porcelain which are scattered around the room. The comfortable seating capacity is eight but it is possible to sit twenty at a pinch. It is an amazing room – even Benjamin Disraeli described it as 'fantastic' after seeing it on his first visit.

Next door is one of the most interesting rooms: the India Room, a small chamber with cabinets around the walls containing examples of every weapon used during the British Raj in India. The room is now used as an office by the Defence Services Secretary, a senior officer seconded from one of the three services in rotation to liaise between the monarch and the services.

Another room used by The Queen for her private luncheon parties is the 1844 Room, so named because it was during that year that it was occupied by Emperor Nicholas I of Russia. The colour scheme of the 1844 Room is white and gold and in honour of its first occupant a special Axminster carpet was ordered which gives the room a very comfortable and cosy atmosphere. It is in this room that The Queen holds meetings of the Privy Council and it is also the room in which foreign ambassadors first present their letters of credence to Her Majesty. The 1844 Room also contains one of the most unusual clocks in the Palace. It is a 'Negress Head' clock in which one of the eyes shows the hours of the day, the other shows the minutes. The eyelids open and close and the pedestal contains a working music box. It is not the most beautiful of works of art but it is certainly interesting and provides quite a talking point.

Visiting Heads of State are normally housed in the Belgian Suite on the ground floor, which overlooks the garden. Like so many of the important rooms and suites in the Palace, this one derived its title from the first person to stay in it; in this case it was King Leopold I of Belgium, Queen

Victoria's uncle. King Edward VIII moved into the Suite when he became King in 1936 because he did not want to live in the Private Apartments which had been occupied by his parents. He made one small change to the domestic arrangements within the Belgian Suite. He had the massive marble bath removed and a shower installed – the first in Buckingham Palace. The suite contains a number of elegant and gracious rooms, including the main reception room called the Regency Room, the Orleans Bedroom, the Spanish Dressing Room and the private dining room known as the Caernarvon Room, after the eighteenth-century Marquess of Caernarvon who was the first person to bring the then Buckingham House to the attention of George III. The Caernarvon Room contains some important Victorian paintings including *The Cousins: Queen Victoria and Princess Victoire, Duchess de Nemours*, painted in 1852 by Winterhalter, Queen Victoria's favourite artist.

The Bow Room is probably the one best known to the outside world, as it is through here that guests to the Royal Garden Parties pass on their way to the Terrace. If you linger long enough you will be able to see the superb Mecklenburg-Strelitz table service, which is arranged in the recesses in the corners of the Bow Room. The service was presented to Queen Charlotte's brother, the Duke Adolphus Frederick IV of Mecklenburg-Strelitz, in 1763 and is said to be the finest example of Chelsea porcelain in existence.

The gardens at Buckingham Palace extend to more than forty acres (16 ha) with a lake at the west end where pink flamingos have delighted the eye since they were introduced in 1959. There are three varieties of rose: 'Queen Elizabeth', 'Silver Lining' and 'Peace', and among the thousands of plants, flowers, shrubs and trees is a black mulberry bearing a label stating that it was planted in 1609 when the Mulberry Garden was formed by James I.

The boundary wall which surrounds Buckingham Palace is topped with barbed wire, which didn't prevent a couple of tourists from climbing over and camping for the night in 1983. They did no harm and no action was taken against them, but the security fences have been strengthened since and there is now an electrified strand on top of the barbed wire and closed-circuit television cameras monitor the entire perimeter.

The Palace has its own cinema, swimming pool and even nuclear fall-out shelter. The unwritten rule for swimming in the pool is that Members of the Household may use it if it is free. If a member of the Royal Family turns up when they are in the pool they may remain in the water, but if a Household Member arrives to find the pool occupied by a royal, they stay out, unless invited in.

In addition to the Royal Mews, described in chapter six, there is one other part of the Palace which is open to the public and that is The Queen's Gallery. The Gallery was built in 1961 and there is a permanent display of selections from the royal works of art, which are changed frequently. The entrance to The Queen's Gallery is in Buckingham Palace Road.

WINDSOR CASTLE

Of the three official residences of the sovereign, two are located in the centre of the great capital cities of London and Edinburgh, while the third, although only twenty miles (32km) from London, is considered to be in the country. Windsor Castle is The Queen's weekend home. She leaves Buckingham Palace at lunchtime on Friday and is driven down the M4 motorway to the Castle, where she stays until Monday afternoon. The Court moves to Windsor in April for the spring break and again for a week in June when Her Majesty hosts a large house party for the Royal Ascot race meeting. It is during this week that the annual Service of the Order of the Garter takes place at St George's Chapel, Windsor. The Royal Family used to spend their Christmas holidays at Sandringham, but since 1964 The Queen has invited all her near relatives to join her and the Duke of Edinburgh at Windsor. Of course the Castle has many memories for both The Queen and her sister Princess Margaret; they both lived there for the six years of the Second World War.

Windsor is the largest inhabited castle in the world and has been occupied continuously since it was built by William the Conqueror. (In 1917, the Prime Minister Lloyd George decided that the Royal Family should get rid of its German surname and adopt a wholly English family name. It was Lord Stamfordham, the King's Private Secretary who suggested the name Windsor, which was immediately accepted. The Castle had been the spiritual home of the monarchy for around 900 years, so what could be more appropriate?) Queen Victoria lived at Windsor for much of the latter part of her life, after her husband Prince Albert died there in 1861. There is a permanent exhibition devoted to the connection between Victoria and Windsor at the town's railway station, with many items which once belonged to Her Majesty on loan by permission of The Queen.

The Castle is one of Britain's biggest tourist attractions and is open to visitors throughout the year. Most enter the precincts through King Henry VIII's Gate, which was built when the Castle was more than 400 years old. This leads into the Lower Ward with St George's Chapel opposite. Immediately to the right of the main gate are the residences of the Military Knights of Windsor, retired army officers who parade in their distinctive scarlet uniforms on ceremonial occasions and play an important part in the services in St George's Chapel.

A fairly steep climb up the hill alongside St George's Chapel brings you to the entrance of the State Apartments, which, unlike most places open to the public, are still very much in use throughout the year.

Although Queen Victoria is the monarch most people associate with Windsor, her contribution to the Castle's physical appearance is confined mainly to the Grand Staircase at the entrance to the State Apartments. It was designed by Anthony Salvin in 1866 and is dominated by a massive marble statue of King George IV, the real influence behind both Buckingham Palace and Windsor Castle. The Grand Staircase leads to the Grand Vestibule in which are displayed many military relics, including the bullet which killed Admiral Nelson at the battle of Trafalgar.

Arguably the most impressive of all the State Apartments is the Waterloo Chamber, another of George IV's schemes. This time it was to commemorate the victory at Waterloo and every year on 18 June, or as near as can be arranged, a banquet is held in the Chamber at which the guest of honour is always the Duke of Wellington. George IV instructed his architect Wyatville to find a suitable gallery to house a large collection of all the monarchs, statesmen and soldiers who had played a part in the decisive victory at Waterloo. The gallery was made by roofing over an open courtyard at the very heart of the State Apartments. This gives the impression of being on board a ship in Nelson's time. There was further restoration added to the room in 1861 on the orders of Queen Victoria and the extensive fretwork which lines the upper walls was incorporated at this time. The intricate woodcarvings are by Grinling Gibbons and the room is dominated by a portrait of the Duke of Wellington in Field Marshal's uniform, wearing the Order of the Garter and holding the Sword of State. The massive table is capable of seating more than sixty guests and on the eve of the Waterloo Banquet it looks truly magnificent, laid with gold plate, priceless china and exquisite floral decorations. The Waterloo Chamber also boasts the largest seamless carpet in Europe, made for Queen Victoria at Agra in India.

St George's Hall is the other great chamber within the State Apartments. Built originally by Edward III, it has been reconstructed twice and its most outstanding characteristic is the multitude of wooden shields on the ceiling, each one bearing the coat of arms of a Knight of the Garter. (There are a few blank shields for the rare occasions when a Knight has been expelled from the Order.) Today the Hall is used for the State banquets given by The Queen to visiting Heads of State.

Alongside the State Apartments is one of the most amazing model houses in the world. It is Queen Mary's Dolls' House, a complete palace in itself, correct in every detail and built to a scale of one-twelfth lifesize. The Dolls' House was designed by Sir Edwin Lutyens and presented to Queen Mary in 1924. The library has works in miniature by noted authors of the day with only one exception. George Bernard Shaw refused to contribute, saying it was a 'gimmick' with which he did not intend to become involved.

The most easily recognisable part of Windsor Castle is the Round Tower, built originally of timber by William the Conqueror and replaced in stone by Henry II in the twelfth century. Today it contains the Royal Archives, a priceless collection of documents and letters belonging to past and present members of the Royal Family. The Archives are not open to the general public but serious students of royal events may apply to see specific items and authors are sometimes granted access to the royal papers as part of their research.

The Private Apartments run along the southern side of the Upper Ward and are never open to the public. The Queen and her Family live on the first floor with the Household offices on the ground floor. The decoration of the Private Apartments is 'country house' style with the accent very much on comfort rather than opulence. The Queen uses the same rooms that were once occupied by her great-great-grandmother Queen Victoria, but instead of the stuffy, dark, over-filled atmosphere of bygone times, the theme today is light and cheerful. It was Queen Mary who was responsible for choosing the gold and white Regency-style decoration, when she had the Private Apartments redesigned in the 1920s. Our present Queen likes the easy informality of Windsor and her sitting room is a cheerful clutter of books, television set, radio, family photos and small statuettes of favourite royal horses – and lots of chintz-covered armchairs. Her Majesty has her own entrance and from her sitting room she can look down the magnificent Long Walk which stretches three miles (5km) across Windsor Great Park; The Queen and her guests form a splendid procession when they ride in carriages down the Walk during Royal Ascot Week. Anyone is allowed to use the Long Walk but only on foot or in a horse-drawn vehicle – no cars are permitted.

The Castle is surrounded by nearly 5000 acres (2025ha) of farm and parkland, including Smith's Lawn where the Prince of Wales plays polo on Sunday afternoons during the season, watched usually by his wife – and about 10,000 spectators.

SANDRINGHAM HOUSE

As soon as the Christmas holiday is over at Windsor Castle, The Queen and the Duke of Edinburgh leave for their estate in the Norfolk country-side to celebrate New Year. Sandringham is one of The Queen's private homes, left to her by her father and bought originally by Queen Victoria as a present for her son, later Edward VII, for £220,000. It is 120 miles (193km) from London and is made of red brick with a grey slate roof, in what is sometimes optimistically described as the 'Elizabethan' style. Realistically it is simply a rambling country mansion designed in the rather pretentious style of many architects of the Victorian period. The 'Big House', as it used to be called by members of the Royal Family earlier this century, looks out over a wide expanse of lawn, with a terrace on the west side descending to a formal sunken garden. The large ornate wrought-iron gates which guard the main entrance to the wide gravel drive were a gift from the people of Norwich. The Queen's father King George VI was born at Sandringham; it was his favourite home during his lifetime, and he died there on 6 February 1952.

There used to be nearly 400 rooms in the house, but in 1965 The Queen decided to demolish ninety-one of them as they were rarely used and would have cost far too much to maintain. The estate extends to over 20,000 acres (8000ha), of which Her Majesty herself farms around 3000 (1200ha) – the rest is let to tenant farmers. Among the houses on the estate is Park House where the Princess of Wales was born during the time her father Earl Spencer was Equerry to The Queen.

Much of the area around Sandringham is open to the public and The Queen is frequently seen walking or riding in the grounds or shopping in the village. On one – now famous – occasion Her Majesty was standing in the village shop when another customer said how like The Queen she looked. The Queen replied, 'How very reassuring', without giving the game away.

BALMORAL CASTLE

Balmoral is the other private home of The Queen, again an inheritance from her father and another of the purchases of Queen Victoria, who, together with Prince Albert, bought it in 1844. There was a small and totally unsuitable castle on the site when Queen Victoria and her consort bought the estate, so they had it demolished and an architect called William Smith from Aberdeen collaborated with Prince Albert to design a new castle in its place. The Castle is situated on the banks of the River Dee in Aberdeenshire, near the town of Ballater where every other shop is able to display the Royal Warrant over its doorway.

The theme of the decoration inside the Castle is tartan. This was chosen by Queen Victoria and has been continued by succeeding sovereigns. There is a number of other houses on the 50,000-acre (20,250-ha) estate including Birkhall, the Queen Mother's residence, and Craigowan, a very pleasant medium-sized country house, which is now mainly used by the Prince and Princess of Wales. Also in the grounds of the Castle is a small wooden chalet, just one room and a kitchen, which was a birthday gift from The Queen to the Duke of Edinburgh. When Lord Wilson of

Rievaulx was Prime Minister, he and his wife were staying as guests at the Castle for the weekend. They were taken to the chalet and while the Prime Minister and His Royal Highness were walking near the river, The Queen and Mary Wilson made the tea and then washed the dishes. There were no servants around and no detectives. Lord Wilson recalls it as one of the most informal occasions of his life. There are not all that many people who can claim to have had tea with the sovereign and then been told to 'clear off while we wash the dishes'.

The Queen spends most of August and September at Balmoral having sailed around the western coast of Britain in *Britannia* in the annual Summer Cruise. The cruise is notable for two events. As the Royal Yacht passes through the Sound of Mull there is an exchange of fireworks with Duart Castle, home of Lord Maclean, the former Lord Chamberlain. As it reaches the Castle of Mey (the Queen Mother's private home on the northernmost tip of the Scottish mainland), the Royal Family always come ashore for a picnic.

Balmoral is regarded by the Royal Family as the most private of all their retreats. Here they can relax and enjoy themselves without having to be constantly on their guard. They can move around the countryside with comparative ease and the locals treat them with the respectful indifference they like. I once asked Princess Anne what her ideal holiday was, in any part of the world. She replied, 'Two weeks at Balmoral with my family.'

THE PALACE OF HOLYROODHOUSE

Once a year, for a week in July, the Court moves to Scotland where the sovereign takes up residence in the Palace of Holyroodhouse in the City of Edinburgh. It is the only occasion when the Court moves out of England and the full majesty, pomp and ceremonial is enacted in the Scottish capital.

The construction of the Palace of Holyroodhouse was begun in 1498 by James IV and was added to by successive sovereigns. Today the Palace includes architecture in the styles of Scottish baronial, early French, Doric arches and elegant Renaissance – with a touch of the twentieth century thrown in with the erection in 1920 of the Edward VII memorial wrought-iron gates which guard the front entrance.

Holyroodhouse shares with Hampton Court Palace the characteristic of having very little furniture. It looks bleak and forbidding from the outside and its interior is hardly more welcoming. The State Apartments are notable mainly for the Picture Gallery, with its romantic associations with Bonnie Prince Charlie who used it for entertaining, and whose walls are hung with no fewer than 111 portraits, all of them ancient Scottish rulers.

The Queen holds a Garden Party in the grounds of Holyroodhouse during the week in July when she is in residence and although the guests dress up as much as their counterparts in Buckingham Palace (with the added charm of national dress) the occasion is much more informal. The Queen's Personal Bodyguard in Scotland, The Royal Company of Archers, is on duty, each member clad in his distinctive green uniform and bonnet, and bands from the Scottish regiments play throughout the afternoon.

CLARENCE HOUSE

The London home of Queen Elizabeth the Queen Mother is probably the most English of all royal homes, set in what is perhaps the most English spot in the world, surrounded by St James's Palace, Buckingham Palace and Marlborough House. It was the first home of the then Princess Elizabeth and the Duke of Edinburgh when they married and Princess Anne was born there. It was Princess Elizabeth who restored much of the house to its original pristine condition, including the magnificent Nash ceiling in the sitting room.

Queen Elizabeth, who has lived in Clarence House since she was widowed in 1952, has brought her own keenly developed artistic sense to its well-proportioned rooms and proved what a natural home-maker she is. In every way, Clarence House, with its Georgian and Victorian memories, is now a superb blend of the past and present. Its many ancient treasures, some inherited with the house (such as the large pictures of former kings and princes, from the Royal Collection) and others from the splendid personal collection begun by Queen Elizabeth in the thirties, are presented in such a way that none has been obscured, nor do any of them conflict with the airy, light decoration that has been the hallmark of its present occupant.

The Queen Mother is a serious collector of silver and china and the quality of the collection becomes immediately apparent to any visitor to Clarence House and reflects the personal taste and character of Her Majesty. Her love of horses is shown in the number of paintings of an equestrian nature adorning the walls and the splendid silver trophies marking the successes she has achieved on the Turf. Queen Elizabeth is one of the most photographed women this century and she has always been a favourite subject for portrait painters, so not surprisingly there is an abundance of likenesses of her looking down in the corridors and reception rooms and she has also spent a great deal of time and effort in locating the pictures and possessions of her Bowes-Lyon ancestors, scouring the sale, rooms and art auctions to find reminders of her Scottish forebears. All are displayed with affection and care, and one other subject who has earned a place of honour in Clarence House is the late

Field Marshal Montgomery. Queen Elizabeth was a great admirer of the leader of the Eighth Army and his photograph is prominently placed in Her Majesty's home.

The Queen Mother has surrounded herself with a staff and Household who are in the main of her own generation. She regards them as friends and the atmosphere inside Clarence House has been described as 'rather like a good country club'. It also has one little extra: a 'blower' – the bookmakers' direct information service which offers the latest prices and winners from all the racecourses. This was installed in 1965 because Her Majesty likes to follow the progress of her horses, even when she cannot get to the racecourse in person. Visitors who are fortunate enough to arrive in the late afternoon or early evening are frequently invited to join Members of the Household for a drink. The only thing you have to be careful of is their size. Clarence House is famous for its extra-large gin and tonics. And if you are very lucky you may be joined by the lady of the house, who is not averse to the occasional aperitif herself.

KENSINGTON PALACE

One of the main advantages of Kensington Palace is that there are so many members of the Royal Family living there in close proximity that security is much less of a problem for the police. At least they are all together in one place, in what has been described as the safest street in Britain – Kensington Palace Gardens – also home for many diplomatic missions, including that of the USSR.

Kensington Palace is a collection of flats and apartments, all of which are on loan from The Queen as 'Grace and Favour' homes. Princess Margaret has her London home there and so too do the Prince and Princess of Wales and their two children; also Princess Alice (The Queen's aunt), the Duke and Duchess of Gloucester and Prince and Princess Michael of Kent. In addition, a number of senior Members of the Royal Household occupy houses within Kensington Palace, notably The Queen's Private Secretary, Sir William Heseltine and her Deputy Private Secretary, Robert Fellowes, who is married to Lady Jane Spencer, elder sister of the Princess of Wales. The Old Barracks, which is part of Kensington Palace, is also used to house Members of the Household. This is a pleasant, roomy building with only one drawback: because it is situated right alongside and practically underneath the giant Kensington Gardens Hotel, it is almost impossible to get a decent television picture.

Kensington Palace was bought from the Earl of Nottingham by William III for the then considerable sum of 18,000 guineas in 1689, because the Palace of Whitehall was prone to flooding in wintertime and Hampton Court Palace was thought to be just that little bit too far out of London.

The mansion needed considerable work and the initial bill paid by the King in 1690 was for £60,000. Even then the work was not finished and in November 1691 a serious fire occurred which meant another £6000 in repair costs and between 1691 and 1696 a further £35,000 was spent in altering 'Kensington House' and the surrounding gardens. It became known as Kensington Palace once the King and Queen moved in and became an official residence of the sovereign. William III died there after he had ordered his servants to carry him from Hampton Court when he knew he was dying after a riding accident.

The Palace's main claim to fame is as the birthplace of Queen Victoria; she was still living there when she learned that her uncle William IV had died and she was Queen. The Court sat at Kensington Palace for just three weeks after Victoria's accession in 1837 before she left for Buckingham Palace, which then became the sovereign's principal London residence (see page 49). This was the last time that Kensington Palace was used as a residence for the sovereign and since then it has become home for a succession of royal relatives. There are a number of State Apartments open to the public, all of which have been preserved in their original condition and furnishings, but there is little danger of any of the present generation of Royals wandering into the public areas – their apartments are well screened and protected on the west side, where they are grouped around a quadrangle known as Clock Court.

ST JAMES'S PALACE

Although no longer a sovereign residence, St James's Palace is still the seat of royal administration and it is to the Court of St James's that all foreign emissaries are accredited. Foreign ambassadors to Britain bring with them Letters of Credence from their governments, establishing their right to represent their country's interests. Incoming ambassadors formally present these Letters to The Queen on their arrival in London, when they also introduce members of their official staff. When their term of office is ended, they take their leave of The Queen in the same way and introduce their successors. This ceremony actually takes place at Buckingham Palace, but because the original Court was in St James's Palace, the accreditation remains to the Court of St James's. It is from the Brick Balcony overlooking Friary Court that the proclamation of a new sovereign is read.

The Palace was once a hospital for female lepers until it was bought by King Henry VIII in 1532. Today the Duke of Kent and his family are the only permanent royal residents – they live in York House. Princess Alexandra and her husband the Hon. Angus Ogilvy also have a small *pied-à-terre* which they use occasionally when they do not have time to return to their home at Thatched Lodge House in Richmond Park.

The main function of St James's Palace these days is as the head-quarters of the Lord Chamberlain's Office. The Queen's personal bodyguard, the Yeomen of the Guard, is also quartered in this Palace and one of the most important offices is that belonging to the Surveyor of The Queen's Pictures. Sir Oliver Millar looks after 5000 pictures in the Royal Collection and he has become the accepted authority on the furniture and decorations of all the royal homes and palaces.

The State Apartments are used by visiting Heads of State to receive members of the Diplomatic Corps and certain Members of the House-hold are permitted by The Queen to hold wedding receptions and other functions amid their ornate and gilded splendour. The Throne Room is the main State Apartment and apart from its use by visiting Heads of State, it has rarely been used since the levees of pre-war days. Although the Palace has been drastically altered since the reign of Henry VIII, one part of the original Tudor building is still visible. It is the four-storey gatehouse which faces straight up St James's Street and outside which sentries stand guard night and day.

St James's Palace is not open to the public during the year and in fact the only opportunity that outsiders have to see the State Apartments is when there is a royal wedding; it is at St James's Palace that the wedding presents are displayed and the entrance fee is donated to charity.

GATCOMBE PARK

The home of Princess Anne and Captain Mark Phillips is far and away the most informal of any of the royal residences. It is also very easy to miss if you have never been there before. As you leave the village of Minchin-hampton in Gloucestershire on the country road that runs due east, the entrance to the estate is on the right-hand side about a mile (1·6km) from the village. But there is no sign to indicate the name of the house and as Gatcombe itself is not visible from the road you could easily miss it – which is exactly how the Princess and her husband like it. They first saw it in 1976, just before they both went to compete in the Olympic Games in Montreal and The Queen bought it for them from the late Lord Butler.

The main house is half a mile (0·8km) along a narrow drive, and just before you reach the house, you come upon a divide in the drive with a signpost directing all traffic to the right. This takes you around the back of the property past a police post which has been skilfully blended in with the surrounding woodland and which is staffed permanently by officers of the Gloucestershire constabulary. If you are expected, however, you will be allowed to drive around to the front of the house where you park on the thinly gravelled terrace, alongside Princess Anne's Scimitar or Captain Phillips's Range Rover.

The first impression I had when I visited Gatcombe is that it was not nearly as big as it appears in photographs. It is beautifully proportioned, but I think the illusion of size is provided by the very large conservatory attached to the front left of the house as you face it. Estimates of what the house cost have been wildly exaggerated, as has the number of rooms. The actual cost was something less than £500,000 and there are thirty rooms in all. Downstairs there is a medium-sized hall containing an old-fashioned rocking horse, a table on which are copies of *Horse and Hound, The Field* and *Riding Monthly* and a litter of wellington boots, old shoes and water bowls which are kept filled for the dogs which roam freely about the place. There is a formal drawing room where official guests are entertained and beyond this is Princess Anne's sitting room, a comfortable room with an elegant bow window, where the Princess sits at her desk writing her speeches and dealing with her correspondence. It is in this room that the Princess and her husband usually take their lunch on trays.

On the other side of the hall is the dining room which can look magnificent when formally set, but which normally has a mountain of papers on its mahogany table dealing with some of Captain Phillips's many business affairs. His study lies beyond the dining room and this is very much a man's room. Deep, comfortable armchairs, a television set with dozens of video cassettes which he says he never gets around to viewing, and a large desk with two telephones.

The kitchen is on the ground floor behind the dining room and it is a typical country kitchen, with not too many modern gadgets. The bedrooms are on the first floor – Princess Anne's has a commanding view over the valley below the house and above is the nursery suite, complete with its own kitchen and bathroom. King George V once said, 'I have a house in London and a home at Sandringham'; Princess Anne simply says, 'My home is Gatcombe.'

HIGHGROVE HOUSE

Just a few miles south of Gatcombe and about a mile (1·6km) outside the market town of Tetbury is the home of the Prince and Princess of Wales. Highgrove House was once considered by Princess Anne and her husband as a possible home before they moved to Gatcombe, but it was rejected for a number of reasons, one of which was security. Although there is a police post at the main gate on the Tetbury road and motorists are discouraged from stopping too close, the house is clearly visible from the main road and there is a public footpath running through the grounds.

However, these were obviously not considered insurmountable obstacles by Prince Charles and neither was the price tag of nearly £1 million. The estate, which contains a farm of some 350 acres (140ha), had been the property of the family of Harold Macmillan, the former Prime Minister. The house has nine principal bedrooms, six bathrooms and a heated swimming pool, plus one other unusual feature for an English country house – a steel-lined room which is said to be impregnable in the event of an attack by terrorists.

The Prince and Princess enjoy living in their Gloucestershire home and spend almost every weekend there, but because they have become the centre of attraction for an unwelcome number of visitors, they rarely venture into the town on informal shopping expeditions as they did when they first moved in. Happily, the locals leave them alone and, apart from relations, they have a number of close friends who live in the area. Prince Charles has now added the farm next door to his property and this is administered by his Duchy of Cornwall estates.

One interesting commercial note. Since the Prince and Princess of Wales moved to Highgrove, property prices in the area have increased enormously. Cottages which were once fetching £10,000 are now being snapped up for as much as £50,000 and the larger houses in a 20-mile (32-km) radius are equally in demand from those who like to claim the Royal Family as neighbours.

DUTY CALLS

It was King George VI who once described the Royal Family as 'the family firm' and the Duke of Edinburgh has since said that living at Buckingham Palace is like 'living over the shop'. In any one year, members of the Royal Family between them will undertake more than 2000 public engagements, with the biggest single contribution coming from The Queen herself who carries out around 500. Buckingham Palace receives more than 50,000 requests for a royal visit every year, and each one is given careful consideration and a polite reply.

Her Majesty's working programme is planned many months in advance, sometimes years if it involves a visit to a foreign country. A check is kept on where The Queen and other members of the Royal Family have been so that there is a fair geographical spread throughout the United Kingdom and overseas. But strangely enough there is not a system of cross-checking within the Palace or between the various Households to make sure that two members of the Family do not turn up at the same place at the same time. On the surface it seems to be somewhat haphazard, but like everything else connected with royalty, it does seem to work. Princess Anne once told me that she had been known to share a helicopter with the Duke of Edinburgh if they happened to be going in the same direction, but it was usually a matter of chance, not planning.

Even when The Queen is not appearing in public, her work continues non-stop. A mountain of paperwork – reports, telegrams and official State papers to be read and acted upon – arrives on her desk every morning, wherever she is, in whatever part of the world.

THE WORKING DAY

The Queen is called at 7.30 a.m. every morning with a cup of tea. Breakfast is at 8.30 a.m. and is usually something simple such as an egg lightly boiled. By 9.30 a.m. Her Majesty is sitting at her desk in her room on the first floor of the North Wing overlooking Green Park. A digest of the day's news has been prepared for her by her Press Secretary, who has read all the national newspapers which are delivered to the Palace. Items of particular interest to The Queen will have been marked or cut out, and important leading articles will be filed for later reference. When Parliament is sitting, Her Majesty also has before her a report on the previous day's proceedings which has been written for her by the Vice-Chamberlain of the Household. This is a political appointment and the holder of the office is a junior member of the government. Lord Home of the Hirsel, the former Prime Minister Alec Douglas-Home, recalls that the report used to be written in the Vice-Chamberlain's own hand, but these days it is typewritten by a secretary and delivered to the Palace on the conclusion of business in Parliament. And it is not a report to be quickly glanced at and then filed away. Lord Home says The Queen always reads it thoroughly and has been known to catch out an unwary Prime Minister whose homework has not been done properly before the weekly audience.

The first daily duty of the three Private Secretaries is to sort out the varied correspondence addressed to The Queen. A great deal is sent to The Queen personally, although much of it has to be dealt with, of necessity, by departments of the civil service and Government, both at home and throughout the Commonwealth. One of Her Majesty's previous Private Secretaries once told me about the sort of letters that arrive at Buckingham Palace every day. These range from the pathetic to the paranoiac: a mother asking for The Queen's intervention on behalf of her son who might have been convicted of an offence; an eccentric demanding the influence of a royal prerogative over some invention they claim has been stolen by an international conglomerate; letters from the plainly crazy offering love, marriage and every other sort of relationship; and petitions from the more responsible and sane population for a wide variety of causes. Invitations by the thousand pour into Buckingham Palace, each one asking for a royal presence at a function to be held weeks, months, in some cases years in advance. And every morning there is always a large bundle of handwritten notes from children, asking The Queen such important questions as:'Did you eat porridge when you were a little girl?' and 'Can I come and sit on the throne?' Yet every single letter that comes to the Palace receives a polite reply – even those from the obviously mad! A number of people write to different members of the Royal Family simply for the thrill of receiving a reply written on the notepaper headed Buckingham Palace.

The mail is divided by the Private Secretaries before The Queen sees any of it. Personal letters to The Queen from friends and family are left unopened and they are recognisable by the fact that they contain the initials of the writer in the bottom left-hand corner of the envelope. Letters which concern The Queen as Head of State are forwarded to the appropriate Government department for action; whatever decision The Queen makes as Head of State it is always as a result of the 'advice' she is given by her ministers. So, for example, if Her Majesty received a petition asking her to intervene on behalf of someone convicted for a crime in the United Kingdom, she would seek the advice of the Home Office (or in the case of the matter coming under Scottish law, the Scottish Office). 'Advice' may be the term used to describe the message passed to The Queen by her ministers, but constitutionally the sovereign is bound by law to accept that advice, and so the actual decisions are taken by the appropriate government ministers. Of course The Queen is now so experienced in constitutional matters that she is able to exercise considerable influence if she so desires and there have been occasions when she has intervened personally because she has been touched by a letter addressed to her.

There are of course many letters which are purely routine and the Private Secretaries know it is unnecessary for The Queen to see these herself, so they will reply on her behalf. The letters from children are usually passed to one of the Ladies-in-Waiting to answer. These generally receive a personal note written in the kind of language not normally found in the formal missives which emanate from Buckingham Palace. If a letter arrives that seems a little out of the ordinary and which the Private Secretaries feel would be the sort of thing The Queen herself would want to see, it is placed before her in a separate pile. Her Majesty will then decide how she wants the reply worded, or occasionally, and this occurs more frequently than most people would imagine, she will even write back in her own hand. I know a lady who wrote to The Queen in 1966 after the mining disaster at Aberfan in South Wales, where more than a hundred children were killed. She had been so impressed by The Queen's actions when The Queen and the Duke of Edinburgh visited the village that she wrote a letter of appreciation. She was amazed and deeply touched to receive, not a formal acknowledgement, but a handwritten letter, several pages long, from The Queen herself.

Apart from the daily post which arrives at the private post office in Buckingham Palace, there are also the official State papers, documents and telegrams which have been brought by messenger from 10 Downing Street, the Foreign Office and all the other Government departments in Whitehall. It has become a well-known fact that The Queen spends several hours of every day 'doing her boxes'. This refers to the communications from Ministers of the Crown that are sent to The Queen in red leather dispatch boxes, several of which arrive every day, wherever The Queen is. The business of monarchy never stops – even if Her Majesty is on board *Britannia*, a helicopter will rendezvous every morning and deliver the mail for The Queen's attention. The contents of the boxes are examined only by The Queen herself – she has one key and the Minister who has sent the box has the other. The Duke of Edinburgh is not privy to official State papers but in recent years the Prince of Wales has been permitted to see some of them as part of his preparation for the time when he becomes king.

The telegrams from the Foreign Office which have arrived in Whitehall throughout the night from all over the world are given special attention, for they give The Queen the information she needs to know concerning the latest state of Britain's relations with other countries. They also usually contain the background to some of the leading foreign news stories she has read in the morning newspapers.

Correspondence from Commonwealth countries is not filtered through any British government department. It either comes direct from the country itself or, more usually, from the offices of the High Commissioners in London. Sir 'Sonny' Ramphal, Secretary-General of the Commonwealth, says that all forty-nine countries within this family of nations are most assiduous in making sure The Queen is kept fully informed of what is happening, including those which are independent republics.

Another of the regular duties of the sovereign – one in which she takes a very personal interest – is the question of the centenary telegrams. One of the most treasured possessions of many families in Britain and the Commonwealth is the telegram sent by The Queen to those celebrating their 100th birthday. Each year some 2000 of these greetings are dispatched and Her Majesty apparently likes to make sure that the messages of congratulation are varied in their content. She does not like the idea of a stereotyped telegram bearing the same words going to all her subjects on this significant milestone in their lives. People sometimes ask how The Queen knows if someone is approaching their 100th birthday. Is she informed officially by the registrar of births, marriages and deaths? Nothing so formal or automatic. The answer is usually that relatives or friends inform the Palace well in advance and to make sure a mistake, intentional or otherwise, is not made, a copy of the relevant birth certificate is required to verify the dates.

The correspondence will take several hours every morning with the remainder of the period before lunch being taken up with visits by a large number of people. In order that The Queen can carry out her many duties as Head of State she needs the assistance of a great many others. One of the most important aspects of The Queen's life is her wardrobe. She appears in public on so many different occasions, and in so many different climates, there is a need for a continual round of fittings and consultations. Obviously it would be impractical for Her Majesty to go to her dress designers' workrooms herself, so they come to her. Then there are the official visitors who have to be received. There are nearly seventy foreign diplomatic missions in London and they are all required to present their credentials to the sovereign on arrival and to take their leave at the end of their posting. The protocol for these occasions has been laid down for many years and is strictly adhered to by every nation, large or small, monarchy or republic. A State coach is sent from the Royal Mews to collect the incoming emissaries who arrive in full Court dress, accompanied by several senior members of their legation. They present their Letters of Appointment to Her Majesty and those recalling their predecessor. It is a formal ceremony that takes place several times every year and the format is always exactly the same. All British ambassadors and Consul Generals are also received by The Queen on taking up their appointment and outgoing diplomats have the right to see The Queen at the end of their term of office.

There may also be a meeting of the Privy Council, the body which is the oldest part of Her Majesty's government, whose origins can be traced back to Norman times. The Privy Council is used increasingly these days because an Act in Council can be made far more quickly than an Act of Parliament. The Privy Council prorogues and dissolves Parliament; it is used for legislation in many international matters such as diplomatic immunity and overseas taxation; there is a Privy Council whenever a member of the Royal Family wishes to get married. The list is long and varied. There are around 300 Privy Counsellors but the usual number attending is four or five. They meet in the 1844 Room at Buckingham Palace, or occasionally elsewhere – they have even held meetings on board *Britannia* – and The Queen receives them standing. Indeed, that is how the entire business of the Privy Council is conducted, with all present standing. The only time a large number of Counsellors is summoned to attend is when The Queen wishes to announce a royal marriage (the Duke of York's engagement in 1986 was the most recent occasion for a mass attendance).

So this is the general pattern of The Queen's working day until lunch, which she usually has alone except for those occasions when there is an official function or when she has invited guests. About a dozen times a year, The Queen and the Duke of Edinburgh give small informal luncheon parties for people from all walks of life. They can be broadcasters, authors, architects, sailors – in fact anybody at all. These lunches are intended to give The Queen a chance to meet and talk informally with a variety of people in a comparatively relaxed and intimate atmosphere. John Snagge of the BBC was once one of those on the coveted guest list – with no idea how or why!

The first indication I had was a telephone call, surprisingly not a formal invitation on printed paper. The call came from the Master of the Household, who wanted to know if I would be free on a certain day because Her Majesty would be pleased if I would take luncheon with her at Buckingham Palace. Naturally I accepted very rapidly. It's the sort of invitation that even if you have other engagements, you cancel everything and go there. I was naturally frightened at the time as to the formality of the occasion and thinking that I must not only be properly dressed but I must behave myself immaculately when I got there. So I went down to Buckingham Palace, was told exactly where I was to go by the policeman at the gate, stepped out of the car in the inner courtyard, to be greeted by someone from the Royal Household who recognised me at once, which was the first surprise, considering we had never met before. I was then led through the Palace to a room at the back overlooking the gardens where I met my fellow guests. We stood around, all feeling slightly nervous and wondering what the next procedure was going to be. The whole thing was made extremely easy by the Members of the Household who seem by some miraculous means to know each of you by name and also your background. Then comes the moment when you are asked to stand in a line to be greeted by The Queen and Prince Philip. The first thing that happens is that the doors are opened and into the room come tearing flat out, three corgis, and they roar across the room barking like mad, followed rapidly by Her Majesty and Prince Philip and everyone who has come to lunch is duly presented. From that moment on, the thing is as completely informal as the invitation. It has got great charm, complete informality and you feel absolutely at home throughout.

When The Queen is in London, she frequently accepts an invitation to carry out a public engagement within the home counties area, usually in the afternoon. Shortly before Her Majesty is due to leave Buckingham Palace, several Members of the Household will gather around the Garden Entrance at the side of the Palace, immediately below the Royal Apartments. They always turn up to see The Queen leave and they invariably congregate around the same entrance when she is due back.

An afternoon engagement can mean a visit to a hospital, the presentation of prizes at a school speech day or the unveiling of a monument. They rarely last more than a couple of hours and then it's back to the Palace once more and another round of discussions with her Private Secretaries or other senior Members of the Household. If there's an important banquet planned, the Master of the Household will go over the proposed menu with Her Majesty; the Keeper of the Privy Purse may want to discuss a major purchase or the Lord Chamberlain may have asked for an audience. Contrary to popular belief, the Lord Chamberlain does not see The Queen on a day-to-day basis. He needs an appointment to see her and this is arranged through the Private Secretary's office. The Crown Equerry is a frequent visitor to The Queen's office, discussing the arrangements for transport to the many functions she attends and sometimes asking about a particular equestrian matter. The Queen has direct telephone lines to all the senior Members of her Household and it can be a bit disconcerting if you are sitting in the office of the Press Secretary to suddenly hear the royal voice coming out of the amplifier saying 'Can you come up for a moment Michael?'

Towards the end of the day there is always another pile of documents to be read, initialled and acted upon. No matter how hard The Queen works at her papers, there is always an inexhaustible supply waiting for her attention. In the main, the evenings are kept free; that means supper, usually on a tray sitting with the Duke of Edinburgh before the television set. It does not always work out that way of course. On many evenings there are further engagements at official dinners, banquets and visits to the theatre which are also usually in the line of duty.

Once a week during the working year there is also the audience with the Prime Minister. This takes place on Tuesday evenings and lasts for about an hour and a half. It is a strictly business meeting with only the two people present and no aides or secretaries. The Prime Minister is not offered a glass of sherry, tea or coffee – this is not a social call in any shape or form. Lord Home of the Hirsel says he used to tell The Queen what had taken place in Parliament during the previous week and then outline what was planned for the coming seven days. He also said he had to be very careful to do his homework, because The Queen had always done hers! As he put it: 'After all, she is now the most experienced statesman [sic] in the world. She has been doing her job longer than any of the ministers who serve her anywhere in Britain or the Commonwealth.' Lord Home remembered one occasion when he discussed a particular problem with Her Majesty to find that she knew more about it than he did, telling him that she had come up against the same problem 'two Prime Ministers before you'. Contrary to what most people might imagine, The Queen's attitude to her Prime Ministers does not alter with their politics. Because of who she is and the way she was brought up, it is a fairly common assumption that her political leanings might be towards the Conservative party. If this is the case, it has never shown itself in her dealings with her Socialist Prime Ministers. In fact she is known to have become friends with both Harold Wilson (now Lord Wilson of Rievaulx) and James Callaghan. Mr Callaghan tells the story of one weekly audience during the summer months 'when the weather was so nice, we left the sitting room and walked around the gardens of Buckingham Palace talking about the flowers and various shrubs and trees'. So it wasn't all heavy political business and affairs of State.

THE WORKING YEAR

The Royal Family's working year is arranged at programme meetings which take place once every six months, usually in June and December, when the multitude of requests for visits is considered, discussed and decisions taken. These meetings are attended by the Private Secretaries, one of the Press Secretaries and frequently one of the Ladies-in-Waiting. A provisional programme is agreed, with the final decision being taken by The Queen herself.

Other members of the Royal Family have their own personal offices where roughly the same procedure is carried out, although in the case of Princess Anne's office, for example, they no longer hold formal programme meetings. Col. Peter Gibbs, her Private Secretary, simply takes the diary into the Princess's room and between them they arrange which of the hundreds of requests they can fit in. The Ladies-in-Waiting are then given the list for the next six months and they sort out between themselves which engagements they will undertake. The Princess is very flexible as far as her Ladies-in-Waiting are concerned and as long as one of them is available she doesn't really mind which one it is.

One mistake frequently made by individuals and organisations wanting a visit by a member of the Royal Family, is to write to Buckingham Palace without specifying who the request is intended for. When this happens a courteous reply is sent advising applicants to write directly to the Private Secretary of the member of the Royal Family they are hoping to see. If a request comes in for The Queen to attend a function that she is unable to accept, the invitation is never passed on to another member of the Family. As a Member of the Household told me: 'We are not in the business of Rent-a-Royal.'

Once a visit by The Queen has been agreed, a letter is written finalising the date and time. Then the royal machinery swings into action with the practised finesse that has been established over many years. If the engagement is in the United Kingdom, a small advance party will carry out a reconnaissance visit some weeks before the day of the proposed visit. The party consists of either the Deputy Private Secretary or the Assistant Private Secretary, the Press Secretary and one of Her Majesty's personal police officers. They go over every step of the proposed route and individual parts of the itinerary are timed to the minute, stop-watch in hand. There are a thousand and one questions to be asked and answered on both sides. In many cases the organisation receiving the royal visit has never been host to a member of the Royal Family before and they rarely know quite what to expect. If the venue is a commercial organisation, great care has to be taken to ensure that The Queen is not placed in a situation in which she might be seen to be endorsing the firm's products. So if a gift is to be offered, as frequently happens at the conclusion of a visit, it must be agreed to beforehand and the Palace has very definite views on what is acceptable and what is not. The Royal Household make sure that Her Majesty is never exploited, although they are realistic enough to realise that the very presence of the monarch is in itself something that can and will be used to enhance the prestige of the company she is visiting. Then there is the question of who is going to be presented to Her Majesty and the positions they will occupy in the line-up. Once this has been agreed, it has to be adhered to; no alterations are allowed. The Private Secretary will want to know something of the background of those who are to be presented so that no one 'unsuitable' will be shaking hands with The Queen. And the very question of shaking hands is explained. On no account should anyone extend a hand to The Queen until she has offered her hand, and while a firm grip is permitted, too much pressure and violent 'hand pumping' is discouraged. Gentlemen are instructed to bow from the neck, while ladies curtsy, and Her Majesty is addressed as Ma'am (to rhyme with Pam).

How much walking will The Queen be expected to do? How long does it take to get from A to B? Is Her Majesty expected to make a speech? If so, the firm's managing director will be asked to provide sufficient information in order that it may be included. Will The Queen sign the visitor's book? Yes, but it has to be a fresh page and must contain only her signature. Will The Queen accept a bouquet of flowers from the Chairman's granddaughter? Yes, provided it is small and unwired. If the visit is to include lunch, the menu is examined in minute detail: there are very definite guidelines on the royal likes and dislikes. The Queen eats very little and only the simplest food should be prepared. If The Queen is to attend a church service, is it permitted to offer her the collection plate? Yes. And if the Duke of Edinburgh is accompanying her, he sometimes is prepared to read the lesson. The most common question asked whenever any member of the Royal Family is expected is: what do we do about providing lavatories? The answer is simple and basic. One should be set aside just in case – and only for the use of the royal visitor.

The Press Secretary will want to know the requirements of the media. How many reporters and photographers are expected? Is it a visit that should be covered by radio and television? If so, what are the best positions? In London, royal events are fairly commonplace and the media knows exactly what they can and cannot do. They know where they are allowed to stand and how close to The Queen and her Family they can get. But in other parts of the country, the visit may be the event of a lifetime, with the local reporters all anxious to share the coverage with the 'big guns' from Fleet Street. Buckingham Palace is fully aware of the needs of the provincial Press and the Royal Family is known to be concerned that regional papers and television get a fair share in royal coverage. In fact they usually get a much better Press in the regions than they do in London, where familiarity has induced a somewhat blasé attitude. The police officer is concerned with the security measures taken to ensure the safety of his royal charge. How close will the crowds be allowed to encroach? What are the best areas for a 'walkabout'? If there are any high buildings overlooking the proposed route, each one will be inspected thoroughly, both at the 'recce' and on the day of the visit.

Once the preliminary visit has been completed and all the questions answered, the royal party returns to Buckingham Palace to work out in detail the arrangements for the big day. There will still be numerous telephone calls between the Palace and the place where the visit is to take place. No query is considered too small or insignificant. Every call and letter is answered by return in the most extraordinary detail and with the exquisite good manners possessed by almost every Member of the Royal Household.

The Private Secretaries' Offices at Buckingham Palace always issue guidelines for those who are to host a royal visit, with the same rules applying generally for most of the Royal Family with one or two exceptions. Princess Anne, for example, doesn't drink alcohol at all. She prefers Coca-Cola with her meals but also likes mineral water to be available. She does not smoke but she raises no serious objections to anyone else doing so in her presence. She never eats shellfish but almost anything else goes. The Prince of Wales should never be offered red wine under any circumstances and usually prefers coffee to tea. He does not like meals to take too long – an hour for lunch is the maximum he will allow, and he dislikes anyone smoking around him. The Princess of Wales likes to meet small children but does not want them to be forced to talk to her if they are shy. As a former kindergarten teacher herself, she knows only too well the problems of the very young. She also prefers to mingle with people informally and chat, rather than have them presented to her in a formal line-up.

If Queen Elizabeth the Queen Mother is expected, hosts are advised to allow a little more time than usual for each segment. Her Majesty has been known to be unpunctual and she likes to dawdle over a visit, chatting in an informal manner. The Duke of Edinburgh is the exact opposite. He insists on sticking rigidly to the agreed timetable, refuses to listen to rambling speeches – he has been known to interrupt if he thinks someone is being a little long-winded – and he becomes annoyed if too much time has been allowed for a particular section. When an engagement involves The Queen, the final programme is submitted to Her Majesty for her approval, and frequently she will make a suggestion or comment to improve the smooth running of the day's events. Her Majesty is now so experienced at every aspect of the working monarchy that she is able at a glance to tell if a programme is viable or not. One of her former Private Secretaries told me that on more than one occasion he had provided a draft programme for a day's visit, only to have The Queen look at it and say, 'If we cut out this part and tack it on to this part, we can save half an hour and see more people.'

Once the final programme has been agreed and approved a copy is circulated to every department involved. On the day of the engagement, a miniature document which has been photographically reduced to fit pockets and handbags is provided to everyone on duty, with one copy for The Queen herself and one for her Lady-in-Waiting. The Lady-in-Waiting plays a very important part in the royal work pattern. She is The Queen's closest companion, travelling in the royal limousine sitting alongside Her Majesty and smoothing the way when they arrive at their destination. She needs to be cheerful, diplomatic and essentially good at getting on with people from all walks of life. While The Queen is naturally being treated as the guest of honour, the Lady-in-Waiting is escorted by one of the other principal hosts and this, of course, can be anyone from a leading civil servant to the wife of the Mayor of a small borough, who may be slightly overwhelmed by the occasion. Lady Susan Hussey has been a Lady-in-Waiting to The Queen for more than twenty-five years and for a time she was 'loaned out' to Princess Anne in the days before the Princess had Ladies-in-Waiting of her own, so she has seen quite a variety of royal events. She also says she has been treated in a variety of ways when she has been accompanying The Queen: 'from contemptuous indifference to tongue-tied awe.'

The day following a royal visit is a busy one for the Lady-in-Waiting. She has to 'write her letters' – part of her duty is to write thank-you letters to all the people responsible for the previous day's events and all the Ladies-in-Waiting like to write these letters personally. They could so easily have a routine thank-you note printed on the Palace's word processors, but that's not the way things are done by those close to The Queen, although with up to twenty letters having to be written some days, it must be a temptation sometimes.

The preparations for an overseas tour are even more detailed and take place many months in advance. When The Queen goes to another country it is usually at the invitation of that nation's Head of State and often it is to attend a specific event. The six-day visit of The Queen and the Duke of Edinburgh to the United States in 1976 was timed to coincide with the bicentennial celebrations of the founding of the American Republic. In the same year Her Majesty went to Canada to open the Olympic Games; on this occasion she was attending in her role as Queen of Canada. For the duration of the State Visit to Saudi Arabia, where Islamic traditions and customs preclude women from taking an active role in public life, The Queen was treated as an 'honorary gentleman' by the King of Saudi Arabia, thereby emphasising that she was a Head of State visiting another Head of State.

The initial steps towards a State Visit involve both the host Head of State and The Queen's representative in that country, which would be either the British ambassador or the High Commissioner, if the country concerned is a member of the Commonwealth. A draft programme is submitted before the advance party makes its 'recce' visit and The Queen's Private Secretary will discuss the details with her before sending one of his deputies off to carry out the preliminary work. Once the programme has been agreed it is printed in a small, pocket-sized booklet called The Blue Book which is carried by everyone connected with the tour and is regarded as 'the bible' for the Royal Household. It lists such details as the exact time of every event of the entire trip and even the clothes to be worn, which are indicated in a special code: U1 is ceremonial day uniform with decorations and medals; U2 is non-ceremonial day uniform; T1 is tropical day dress, slacks, shirt and tie; T2 is the same but with an open-necked shirt. A capital letter T beside The Queen's name indicates that she will wear a tiara. On a major State Visit, Her Majesty will be accompanied by more than thirty attendants. These range from the Ladies-in-Waiting (two of the eight usually travel abroad); pages; footmen; The Queen's hairdresser; one of the royal doctors; a chauffeur (if one of the royal limousines is being taken); clerical staff from Buckingham Palace, to deal with the multitude of paperwork that follows Her Majesty wherever she goes; security officers; the Assistant Private Secretary who has carried out the 'recce', to make sure everything is as he planned it, and The Queen's Private Secretary, who always accompanies her when she is abroad.

In addition, the Foreign Secretary or one of his ministers may be attached to the Royal Suite for part or the whole of the visit. State Visits are almost invariably timed to coincide with important trade talks or other diplomatic discussions, and frequently these meetings take place on board the Royal Yacht *Britannia*, which The Queen places at the disposal of her government officials.

Among the many items which are carried whenever The Queen pays a visit to a foreign country are the gifts she gives to her hosts and to the people who have worked to make the arrangements for the tour. There is always a costly present for the Head of State, who in turn gives Her Majesty something of great value, though not all can match the generosity of the King of Saudi Arabia, whose gift of jewels is said to be worth several million pounds. Among the more unusual presents was a baby crocodile given to her in The Gambia in 1961. It came in a biscuit tin and spent the night in the bath watched over by a member of the royal entourage. Every present received by The Queen and the Duke of Edinburgh is catalogued and found a home in one of the royal residences, and when the donor visits Britain it is always placed in a prominent position so that he or she can see how much it is valued.

The Queen is aware of how much hard work goes into the preparation of overseas visits and she likes to show her appreciation of these efforts by giving personal mementoes to those who have been involved with the arrangements. These usually take the form of signed photographs of herself and her husband in handsome silver gilt or leather frames; specially designed cuff-links bearing the royal cypher; similarly engraved brooches for ladies; cigarette lighters and wallets. Her Majesty makes sure that she hands over each gift personally with a word of thanks at the end of an engagement.

Every year since her coronation in 1953, The Queen has travelled overseas on official visits. She is the most widely travelled monarch the world has ever known and she has seen and met more of her people than all of her predecessors put together. During The Queen's absence from the United Kingdom, Counsellors of State (appointed by her) act on her behalf. Under the present arrangements, there are six: the Duke of Edinburgh, Queen Elizabeth the Queen Mother and the four adults next in line of succession: the Prince of Wales, the Duke of York, Prince Edward and Princess Anne. Any two of them are eligible to sign official documents requiring the sovereign's signature and to carry out certain other duties in the United Kingdom and the Commonwealth. They do not have the power to dissolve Parliament (except on the sovereign's instructions) and neither are they able to create peers. However, they do carry out investitures on behalf of The Queen.

While she is away with part of the Royal Household, other Members remain in Britain preparing for the domestic programme which always has to be fitted in around the 'static engagements' or the 'hardy annuals'. These are the fixed public occasions which The Queen attends year after year such as: the Royal Maundy (the day before Good Friday); the Service of the Order of the Garter (June); Royal Ascot (June); the Sovereign's Birthday Parade, also known as Trooping the Colour (June); Royal Garden Parties (July); the State Opening of Parliament (November); the Festival of Remembrance and Remembrance Sunday (November). All The Queen's engagements, both at home and overseas, have to be fitted in around these 'immovable feasts' and then there is always the paperwork. The 'boxes' arrive daily to be worked on by Her Majesty in the morning and again in the evening. She cannot leave them until the next day if she is feeling tired – another lot is already on its way. This is one job that cannot be delegated, and even if it could, The Queen would never do it. She realises only too well the importance attached to the handwritten legend 'Approved, E.R.' in the corner of an official document. So if you happen to be walking along Constitution Hill one evening and see a light shining in the only first-floor bow window, it will probably be The Queen, sitting at her desk, surrounded by family photographs, with the little statuette of Princess Anne on Doublet in pride of place, doing what she has reportedly done every evening since 6 February 1952 – working.

STATE OCCASIONS

The ceremony and pageantry which surrounds the monarchy of Britain is a vital element in its enormous appeal. Even though there are those who dislike what they would term the 'ostentatious displays of outdated ceremonial', there is little doubt that the sight of The Queen and members of her Family at the head of a glittering military parade or riding in one of the illustrious State coaches forms one of the most memorable spectacles of the year. There is also little doubt that the magnificent State occasions would not be the same without the historic Regalia which accompanies them.

THE ROYAL REGALIA

The Crown Jewels of England represent one of the most important and valuable collections of precious stones in the world. The questions most commonly asked by the millions of visitors who come to see them in the Tower of London are, firstly, are they real, and secondly, how much are they worth? The answer to the first question is easy: yes, they are and most of them have been worn by the Kings and Queens of Britain for hundreds of years. It would be impossible to answer the second question accurately without taking each individual item separately and having it valued – and this has never been done. Also the intrinsic value of the stones themselves would bear no relation to the historic value of the settings. The Black Prince's Ruby, which is in reality not a ruby at all but a balas or spinel, a semi-precious stone, was once sold for £4 and was worn by Henry V at the Battle of Agincourt. How can you put a price on something like that? Then there is the largest diamond in the world, the First Star of Africa, set in the Sceptre and dated 1661. It weighs 530 carats and the *Financial Times* valued it in 1985 at 'something in excess of £40 million'. The Crown Jewels also contain the Second Star of Africa, which is set in the Imperial State Crown, and the two diamonds clip together to make a brooch. The last time they were worn together in this way was in 1910 by Queen Mary. So really, the Crown Jewels can truly be said to be priceless. They cannot be sold and if they could, who would have the money to buy them?

They are kept in the Jewel House in the Tower of London where they came for the first time in 1216, but only for a temporary stay. Until then they had always been stored at Westminster Abbey, but Henry III removed them to the Tower while part of the Abbey was being rebuilt, then he moved them back again. They remained in the Abbey until 1303 until the night when a thief named Richard de Podnecott attempted to steal them. He was caught, put in the Tower along with the Abbot and several of the clergy, and the lot of them were hanged. King Edward I decided that the Abbey was no longer a safe place to house England's most precious treasures and from that time they have been kept in the Tower of London.

The most famous piece in the entire collection is St Edward's Crown, the Crown of England. It is worn only once in every reign and then only very briefly at the actual moment of coronation. It is the heaviest crown in the collection and is made of solid gold set with semi-precious stones. The present St Edward's Crown dates from the coronation of Charles II, but records held at the Tower show that even then it was an old crown which had been refurbished and from the weight and costs shown in the earliest records, experts believe that at least the lower half of the crown is probably that of Edward the Confessor.

The Imperial State Crown is perhaps the most easily recognised of the Crown Jewels, because this is the Crown The Queen wears on major State occasions such as the State Opening of Parliament. Her Majesty also wore it when leaving Westminster Abbey after her coronation and the Keeper of the Jewel House, Brigadier Kenneth Mears, described it as 'her going away hat'. Altogether it contains some 2800 diamonds and other precious stones, including a sapphire said to have come from the ring of Edward the Confessor; the Black Prince's Ruby; the Second Star of Africa, which weighs 317 carats, and the Stuart Sapphire of some 170 carats. There are also four large, old, drop pearls with quite a romantic background. They were originally given by Pope Clement VII to Catherine de Medici and passed from her to Mary Queen of Scots. When Mary was executed, Elizabeth I bought them and they have passed in succession right down to our present Queen. The Imperial State Crown was designed for Queen Victoria in 1837. It then was altered a hundred years later for the coronation of George VI and again reduced in height in 1953 for Queen Elizabeth II's coronation.

Among the other crowns on display in the Jewel House is the Imperial Crown of India 1911, better known as the Durbar Crown. It was specially made for the Durbar held in Delhi in 1911 when all the Indian princes and maharajahs gathered at a massive public levee in honour of King George V, Emperor of India. Constitutionally none of the crowns of England are allowed to leave the country, so before King George V travelled to India in 1911, the maharajahs sent 6000 precious stones to England, where they were made into the Imperial Crown of India so that the Emperor would not appear before the maharajahs without a crown. The crown travelled back to Delhi for the Durbar, where it was worn on only this single occasion. Since then it has remained in the Tower of London and it is still the most valuable crown in the world.

The crown of Queen Elizabeth the Queen Mother is probably the prettiest of all and it is certainly the favourite of Brigadier Mears. He says it has got 'class'. Made for her of platinum in 1937 for the coronation of King George VI, its principal diamond is the most famous of all precious gems, the Koh-i-noor (Mountain of Light). Weighing originally some 787 carats it has been reduced over the centuries to its present weight of 106 carats and because it is considered unlucky for a man to wear it, it is always placed in the Queen Consort's crown.

The Small Crown of Queen Victoria gives a wonderful indication of how tiny a woman she was. It was made in 1870 because it was said the Queen disliked the Imperial State Crown believing it made her look 'top heavy'. The Small Crown only weighs 4 ounces (125 g) and to wear it, a bun hair-style, as favoured by Queen Victoria, is required.

Queen Mary's Crown is very simple and elegant. Made in 1911 for her husband's coronation, its most outstanding characteristic is the large, oval crystal set in the centre of the Maltese cross at the front of the crown. This crystal can be interchanged with the far more valuable Koh-i-noor diamond if the occasion demands. At one time the third and fourth largest stones of the Cullinan Diamond were also set in this crown but they too have been replaced by crystals and the diamonds have returned to the personal possession of The Queen.

There are three crowns which have not been worn for many years and are unlikely ever to be worn again. They are: the Crown of Mary of Modena made in 1685 and measuring only five inches (12·5 cm) across (last worn by Queen Charlotte, wife of George III); the Prince of Wales' Crown of 1728, made for the son of George II (last worn by King Edward VII when he was Prince of Wales); and the Prince of Wales' Crown of 1901, which was made to be worn by Edward VII's son Prince George (later King George V) and was last worn by the late Duke of Windsor as Prince of Wales at the coronation of his father King George V in 1911.

Among the coronation Regalia, two of the oldest pieces are the Ampulla and the Spoon. The Spoon dates from the twelfth century and was used at the coronation of King John in 1199, or at least part of it was: probably the handle which is some sixty to eighty years older than the bowl. The Ampulla is in the form of an eagle and it holds the anointing oil which is poured out of the beak. It is an interesting item because the head and the body come from different centuries. The body was made for the coronation of Charles II in the seventeenth century, but experts have decided that the head's screw thread dates from the fourteenth century. One theory is that when Cromwell disposed of the Crown Jewels (even though he had a crown for himself) an enterprising clergyman pocketed the head after selling the body, which was the most valuable part of the Ampulla. Then, on the restoration of the monarchy in 1660, the head was produced and a new body was made to fit it.

Another item used as an integral part of every coronation service is the Coronation Ring, often called the Wedding Ring of England. Until the time of William IV and Queen Adelaide, new rings were made for every coronation, but since then the same ring has been worn by every sovereign with the exception of Queen Victoria. Her fingers were too small for the ring so another one was made, but this time the jeweller made it for the wrong finger. There are two ways of counting the fingers on the hand; one is to start with the thumb and the other to start with the index finger which is what the jeweller did. When the time came for the Archbishop to place the ring on Queen Victoria's hand there was great difficulty in forcing it on to the third finger, as it had been made for the little finger. However, the Archbishop persevered, causing great discomfort to Her Majesty, who then had to spend two hours after the ceremony trying to remove the ring. That is why we have two sovereign's rings on show today.

Whenever we see a picture of The Queen at her coronation it usually shows her with the Orb in one hand and the Sceptre in the other. The Orb is the emblem of sovereignty and dates from the time of Charles II. (There is also a smaller one which was made for the unique double coronation of William and Mary. William, invited by the government to succeed his uncle James II when the latter became a Roman Catholic, married Mary, James II's daughter and rightful heir to the throne. Each was sovereign in their own right, so two orbs were necessary.) The Orb is a hollow ball of gold, six inches (15 cm) across, encircled by a gold band decorated with diamonds and other precious gems and edged with pearls. It weighs two pounds and four ounces (1 kg). The Sceptre with the Cross was made for the coronation of Charles II but redesigned in 1910 to accept the First Star of Africa diamond, the largest gem in the world. This Sceptre symbolises the sovereign's temporal power as ruler while the Sceptre with the Dove is said to represent the sovereign's authority as the source of justice and mercy. The sovereign's Personal Sword of State is the most valuable sword in the world. It has a solid gold scabbard and is inlaid with magnificent jewels. It was made for George IV in 1821 and cost £5998. Translated into modern terms that would obviously mean millions. The government of the day were so incensed by the cost that they refused to pay for it, so the King footed the bill himself. Ironically, at every coronation it is redeemed for the sum of 100 shillings (see page 85).

The Coronation Robes are also kept in the Tower of London where they are displayed on the ground floor of the Jewel House. The Imperial Mantle and the Supertunica (also called the Pallium or Robe Royal of Cloth of Gold) were both made for George IV in 1821. They are of gold thread and are very heavy indeed, weighing twenty-three pounds (10 kg). Together they are so bulky that Queen Victoria was unable to wear them at her coronation in 1838, but our present Queen followed her father and wore all the Regalia. The newest part of the Regalia is the Stole which was made specially for The Queen in 1953. It was presented by the Commonwealth nations of which she was then Head and contains emblems of those countries. Together with the thirteen Maces, the Spurs, Armills, Communion Plate and Christening Fonts, the Crown Jewels are a representation of the continuity of the monarchy in Britain. They are seen by millions of people from all over the world who wonder at their beauty – and value! One thing most of them don't know, however, is the fact that not a single item is insured. As Brigadier Mears puts it: 'How can you insure something that's irreplaceable?'

THE CORONATION

The most important of all State occasions is of course the coronation, partly by virtue of the fact that it happens only once in every reign. The unchanging continuity of the coronation service through the centuries lends a peculiar characteristic that is all its own. The basis of the service which saw Elizabeth II crowned in Westminster Abbey on 2 June 1953 was very much the same as that devised by St Dunstan for the coronation in the year 973. The coronation is a religious service and the actual moment of crowning is only a brief interlude. The English constitution rests firmly on the Christian faith and tradition, and the coronation consists largely of the Holy Communion service of the Church of England. The anointing of the sovereign with holy oils is the basis of the ceremony, traditionally associated within the Church as the mark of consecration, while the oath is a further public proclamation of the sovereign's contractual obligation to govern all his or her peoples, administer law and justice and uphold the faith of the Church of England.

Of course one major difference in the ceremonial from St Dunstan's day was the fact that the coronation in 1953 was the first to be filmed and televised live. This is a commonplace occurrence today for most State occasions, but even in those comparatively recent times the impact was monumental. Television during the post-war years was still in its infancy. Sets were restricted to less than 2000 in Britain and most of those were in the areas immediately around London. At first Her Majesty wasn't all that enthusiastic about allowing cameras into Westminster Abbey and most of her advisers, including the Archbishop of Canterbury, were equally opposed. Sir Winston Churchill was also suspicious of the new medium of television but eventually, realising that here was an opportunity not to be missed, agreed to the proposal and persuaded The Queen accordingly.

Westminster Abbey, the scene of so much royal ceremonial, has become accustomed to the participation of the media. In fact the Precentor, the Reverend Allan Luff, who looks after the musical aspect of all royal services at the Abbey, enjoys the challenge posed by the presence of the television cameras. He says:

We are learning to look on the media not as an intrusion but as an opportunity. Before, we laid out the Abbey just for the few hundred who could actually see what was going on and the rest (in the nave) who could only hear; now we are able to present things in a much more exciting way visually, which we would never have done before. We are now getting used to thinking 'television wise'.

It may be interesting to note that without television cameras, only the 1800 guests the Abbey can accommodate would have any idea of what is going on, and of those, only about 200 who sit immediately in front of the high altar can actually see the events taking place. The only view the remainder have is of the royal processions as they enter and leave the Abbey. So television monitors are installed at strategic points, in order that those inside the Abbey church can see as well as those watching at home.

When The Queen was crowned in Westminster Abbey on 2 June 1953, it was before a congregation of nearly 8000 people (special galleries were built to accommodate the extra numbers) and three-quarters of a million people lined the streets of London to watch the processions to and from the Abbey. The solemnity and pageantry of the service dated back a thousand years and was as splendid and emblematic in the twentieth century as it had been at any time in the history of England. The responsibility for the arrangements rested with the Earl Marshal, the Duke of Norfolk, who as the premier earl of Britain is Head of the College of Arms, and it was he who was the first to greet The Queen when she arrived at Westminster Abbey.

Nearly a year before the coronation took place, on 7 June 1952, a royal proclamation announced that a date had been set for the coronation. In language both archaic and majestic, it was read from the Brick Balcony at Friary Court in St James's Palace by Garter Principal King of Arms; also at Charing Cross by Lancaster Herald; at Temple Bar by Norroy and

Ulster King of Arms; and at the Royal Exchange by Clarenceux King of Arms. The identical passage was also read in principal cities throughout the United Kingdom and the Commonwealth.

On coronation eve, the royal Regalia was brought to Westminster Abbey, and early on the day it was carried in procession through the cloister to the high altar.

When The Queen arrived at the west door of the Abbey she was met by the procession which had formed to accompany her. Taking part were the Archbishops and Bishops; representatives of the Church of Scotland and of the Free Churches; the Standard Bearers; the Barons of the Cinque Ports; the four Knights of the Garter who had been selected to hold the silken pall over The Queen while she was being anointed; the Prime Minister of the United Kingdom and those of the Dominions; the Heralds and Pursuivants; the Peers who had responsibility for carrying the Regalia and all the others who had a part to play in this, one of the greatest royal ceremonials in the world. The Regalia was borne immediately before Her Majesty: the St Edward's Staff, the Sceptre with the Cross, the two Golden Spurs, the five Swords of State, the Sceptre with the Dove, and the Orb, each carried by a Peer of the Realm attended by a page. Then followed the most important piece in the entire Regalia, St Edward's Crown, borne on a velvet cushion by the Lord High Steward, attended by two pages. The chalice, the paten and the Bible, each carried by a Bishop, completed this part of the Royal Procession.

The centrepiece of the coronation service is the 'theatre', a platform built in the middle of the Abbey before the high altar. As the royal Regalia was placed on the altar, The Queen spent a few moments in private prayer before the service began. The coronation service itself is basically the religious celebration of Holy Communion with the addition of the Crowning. There are five distinct parts: the Recognition, the Oath, the Anointing, the Investiture and the Homage.

The Recognition
First of all The Queen was formally presented to those in the Abbey. As she turned herself to each of its four corners, the Archbishop of Canterbury spoke the following words:

Sirs, I here present unto you Queen Elizabeth, your undoubted Queen. Wherefore all you who are come this day to do your homage and service. Are you willing to do the same?

Each time the reply from the congregation was the same: 'God Save Queen Elizabeth.'

The Oath

The Archbishop of Canterbury then asked the questions contained in the Order of Service which include demanding of The Queen that she uphold the laws and justice of Britain and the Commonwealth and, as Defender of the Faith, maintain the established Protestant Church. When these questions had been answered The Queen was led to the altar, where, kneeling, she laid her right hand on the Bible and took the coronation oath, kissed the book and signed a transcript of the oath.

The Anointing

For this part of the ceremony The Queen removed her crimson robe, her diadem and the Collar of the Garter as a sign of humility. Clad in a simple white gown she was escorted to St Edward's Chair where she sat while four Knights of the Garter held a gold canopy over her during the anointing. The oil was poured from the Ampulla into the Anointing Spoon and the Archbishop of Canterbury anointed The Queen in the form of a cross. Then The Queen proceeded to a faldstool where she knelt as the Archbishop pronounced the blessing.

The Investiture

This is the sequence where The Queen is invested with the symbols of her office: the Spurs, the Sword of State, the Armills, the Orb, the Ring and the Glove, the Sceptre, the Rod.

The Spurs are a symbol of chivalry and when the sovereign is a man, they are either worn or the heels are touched. In the case of The Queen, she laid a hand on them as a token of acceptance before they were returned to the altar.

The Sword of State was delivered by the Lord who carried it, to the Lord Great Chamberlain, who deposited it in St Edward's Chapel. Another sword in a scabbard was laid upon the altar by the Archbishop who prayed that Her Majesty would use it as the minister of God. The sword was placed in The Queen's hands with the words: 'With this sword do justice.' Then The Queen went to the altar and offered the sword in its scabbard. The Peer who first carried it offered the price of it, namely 100 shillings, and having redeemed it, received it from the Altar, drew it out of its scabbard and thereafter carried it unsheathed before Her Majesty during the rest of the ceremony.

The Armills were fastened on to The Queen's wrists, one to symbolise wisdom, the other sincerity. Then she was invested with the Stole Royal and the Pallium or Robe Royal of Cloth of Gold. The Orb was then placed in The Queen's right hand as a symbol of Christian sovereignty over the earth, the sovereign being head of the Anglican Church. The

Sovereign's Ring was then placed on the fourth finger of Her Majesty's right hand with the words of presentation and the Glove was also placed on the same hand. Following the Glove and the Ring, The Queen was invested with the two Sceptres, one with the Cross and the other with the Dove and once The Queen had been invested with these symbols of her office, all was ready for the climax of the coronation service – the moment of crowning.

The Archbishop placed St Edward's Crown on The Queen's head and the sovereign was acclaimed by the congregation with cries of 'God Save The Queen'. The Princes and Princesses and the Peers and Peeresses put on their coronets, the trumpets sounded a fanfare and at a signal, the guns in the Tower of London and Hyde Park fired a royal salute.

The Queen wore St Edward's Crown for only a short time, which was just as well because it weighs just an ounce under five pounds (2·2 kg). She left St Edward's Chair and for the first time ascended her throne from where she received the Homage of her leading subjects. The Duke of Edinburgh, removing his coronet, knelt before The Queen and placing his hands between The Queen's, swore his words of homage, followed by the Duke of Gloucester and the Duke of Kent. The royal Dukes each kissed The Queen on the left cheek while the other Peers of the Realm kissed her right hand.

The Communion followed the Homage in which Her Majesty offered her oblation, an altar cloth and a gold ingot weighing one pound (0·5 kg). Having removed St Edward's Crown to be replaced by the much lighter Imperial State Crown and the Royal Robes of Gold for one of purple velvet, Her Majesty retained the Orb and Sceptre and the Royal Procession left Westminster Abbey. The ceremony, which had lasted three hours, had basically remained unchanged for nine centuries.

The procession which formed to escort The Queen back to Buckingham Palace was two miles (3·2 km) long and took three-quarters of an hour to pass any given point. The route had been devised to give as many people as possible an opportunity of seeing the newly crowned Queen. It ran from Westminster Abbey, across Parliament Square into Whitehall, then up past Downing Street and into Trafalgar Square, where a quarter of a million people had waited, some of them for more than twenty-four hours. It then went from Trafalgar Square west along the length of Pall Mall, passing St James's Palace on the left as it turned up into St James's Street; then Piccadilly, East Carriage Drive and into Oxford Street travelling east and passing Selfridge's on the left, dressed as only one of London's most famous stores knew how, with every window depicting some aspect of royalty through the ages. (Above the main entrance was a lifesize statue of The Queen on horseback and behind that a huge portrait of the first Queen Elizabeth, flanked on either side by huge scrolls containing the proclamations of both sovereigns.) Then the procession moved into Oxford Circus and along the elegant shopping façades of Regent Street, before rounding Piccadilly Circus, where the famous statue of Eros appeared in a gilded cage fully fifty feet (15 m) high. They then turned into the Haymarket, where the decorations included standards surmounted by features such as Household Cavalry helmets, and once more back around Trafalgar Square, under the Admiralty Arch and into The Mall for the final mile (1.6 km) before Buckingham Palace. Over The Mall appeared three ceremonial arches sixty-five feet (20 m) in height, each having a design of lions and unicorns on top and a princess's coronet suspended beneath. The atmosphere in London that day was full of excitement: the crowds sang and danced, every policeman and soldier who passed was given a cheer and when The Queen and the royal procession appeared the noise was deafening. The Earl Marshal and the Lord Chamberlain had measured the distance exactly: it was five miles 250 yards (8·3 km) and it took Her Majesty one hour and forty minutes to travel. People had crowded into London from all over the world and the festivities continued long into the night until dawn. At night London took on a glitter of its own as all the main public buildings were illuminated by floodlights and there were street parties celebrating throughout the capital and the length and breadth of the country.

THE QUEEN'S BIRTHDAY PARADE

The only occasion when Her Majesty appears in public on horseback is on her official birthday, usually the second Saturday in June, when The Queen's Birthday Parade takes place at Horse Guards. The event is generally, but mistakenly, known as Trooping the Colour, but this is just a part of the two-hour Parade and not its entirety. It is in fact a combination of two very ancient drills, Trooping the Colour and Mounting The Queen's (or King's) Guard, and each move in the intricate display of marching and counter-marching has been passed down by word of mouth from generation to generation. Some of the manoeuvres are so complicated they would be impossible to write down, but year after year they are always perfectly performed. Among all the pageantry and ceremonial of Britain's monarchy, the sovereign's Birthday Parade ranks among the year's truly great occasions and attracts thousands of people from all over the world. It is also regularly seen live on television by millions more.

The reason for an 'official birthday' originated in the days of Queen Victoria, whose birthday was 24 May. The Queen spent the month of May at Balmoral so it was decided to celebrate her birthday 'officially' in June when the Court returned to London. King Edward VII, who was born on 9 November 1841, decided that, because the weather at that time of year in Britain is always so inclement, it would be in everyone's interests to retain the custom of an official birthday in June, when at least there was a chance of better weather. The 'official birthday' tradition has remained ever since.

The Queen rides at the head of her regiments (accompanied by the royal Dukes, who are honorary Colonels-in-Chief of Guards Regiments) from Buckingham Palace down the tree-lined avenue of The Mall and into Horse Guards Parade, arriving exactly as the clock strikes eleven – although rumour has it that on occasion the clock has been timed to strike as The Queen arrives and not the other way round!

Like nearly every other aspect of British ceremonial and pageantry, the Birthday Parade and Trooping the Colour have their roots deep in military history. The term 'trooping' means 'saluting by beat of drum' – hence the significance of that instrument in The Queen's Birthday Parade. Although Trooping the Colour is now regarded as one of the most exciting spectacles in the royal calendar and one of the biggest tourist attractions in the world, there was a very practical origin to the custom. England's first official Standing Army was formed several centuries ago and it was important that the soldiers recognised who they were fighting for. Mercenaries were commonplace, and many of the soldiers who signed up to fight for England couldn't speak a word of English, so a visual rallying emblem became their point of focus; the standard (or 'colour') of their regiment would be paraded through the lines of the troops every night before a battle, just to remind them which side they were on. The music which accompanied the Trooping was especially chosen to instil a sense of fighting camaraderie and to boost morale. What has now become a pleasant attraction for the spectators at the Birthday Parade was in fact an integral part of the day's proceedings with a practical purpose.

Altogether, more than 2000 men and 200 horses take part in the ceremonial, including detachments of the mounted regiments of the Household Cavalry and the Massed Mounted Bands. Her Majesty is the only woman on parade. The Queen is Colonel-in-Chief of all seven regiments of the Household Division: the foot guards – the Irish, Scots, Welsh, Coldstream and Grenadier Guards; and the two cavalry regiments – the Life Guards, which is the senior regiment in the British army, and the Blues and Royals, which was formed by amalgamating the Royal Horse Guards and the Royal Dragoons. The colour to be trooped is selected by rotation and The Queen appears on parade wearing the tunic of that regiment, as well as a tricorn hat decorated with its particular badge and plume.

Her Majesty is in no way merely a figure-head and she plays an active part in the two-hour ceremony. She is known to take particular notice of the standard of drill and the turnout of the guardsmen on parade. Nothing escapes her eye and several officers have been disconcerted shortly after a Birthday Parade to receive a note from The Queen, remarking on something or someone who has not been up to the standard she expects, although this does not apply when guardsmen faint on parade.

The Queen is usually the most experienced person on parade. She has taken part in every Birthday Parade since the coronation, far more than any of her officers or guardsmen, and her own impeccable standards of discipline and horsemanship were superbly demonstrated in 1981, when she magnificently brought her horse under control after a youth in the crowd had fired blank cartridges at her.

On the morning of the Parade, when The Queen's horse Burmese is being prepared for the ceremony, those men taking part will have been up and about since long before dawn, polishing buttons and boots and brushing their bearskins; the mounted troopers have to groom their horses, which sometimes appear to have been given even more attention than their riders.

By 10.30 a.m. those fortunate enough to have been allotted one of the 7000 tickets available must be in their places (they have to have a ballot every year because around 100,000 people apply). Eight contingents of foot guards, each consisting of three officers and seventy other ranks, are formed up across the parade ground. The Massed Bands of the Guards Division, together with the Corps of Drums and the Pipes and Drums parade in front of the garden wall at the rear of 10 Downing Street, which backs on to Horse Guards. Queen Elizabeth the Queen Mother, with other members of the Royal Family, is then driven on to Horse Guards. The national anthem is played after which they move to the Horse Guards Building to watch the proceedings from the Major General's office above the centre archway. The moment of the arrival of the sovereign is marked by the playing of the national anthem once more and the firing of a forty-one-gun royal salute by the King's Troop Royal Horse Artillery in nearby Hyde Park.

As The Queen passes beneath the window where Queen Elizabeth is watching, she always gives her mother a salute which is returned with a smile and a wave. Then the first duty of the sovereign is to ride slowly through the ranks of the foot guards inspecting them in a Royal Review. She then returns to the saluting base, where she remains sitting motionless on horseback for the remainder of the Parade – nearly an hour and a half!

The Massed Bands give a display of marching and counter-marching in slow and quick time, always beginning with the traditional slow march

'Les Huguenots'. Once they have re-formed at their original places, a lone drummer beats 'Drummers Call' as an indication that Trooping the Colour is about to begin. The Regimental Sergeant Major, carrying a drawn sword on the only ceremonial occasion he is allowed to do so, hands over the colour to the youngest Ensign in the regiment, who will carry it for the rest of the ceremony. The colour is extremely heavy, so most young officers who know they are going to be bearing it go into strict weight training for several weeks prior to the Parade, to become fit enough to support it during the lengthy ceremony. The colour, having been handed to the Ensign, is now trooped down the lines of guards, while the Massed Bands perform the most complicated movement of the entire parade – the spin-wheel technique, a secret handed down by each Drum Major to his successor. Over the past 150 years the manoeuvre has scarcely varied.

Once the colour has been trooped through all the ranks, the soldiers form up to march past The Queen, again in slow and quick time. As the colour passes Her Majesty it is lowered in slow time and it is at that moment that those weeks of weight training prove themselves.

After the Household Cavalry has trotted past the saluting base, The Queen places herself at the head of her Guards and leads them off Horse Guards Parade, back along The Mall to Buckingham Palace. The first two divisions go to the forecourt of the Palace to become the new guard, while the rest of the Parade marches past The Queen for the final time. For The Queen it has been a morning of complete discipline, sitting for more than two hours in a position that could never be described as comfortable. According to the late Lord Mountbatten, however, her first thought as she dismounts is for her horse. Burmese is always given a lump of sugar as a reward and then Her Majesty joins other members of the family on the balcony of Buckingham Palace for the traditional flypast by aircraft of the Royal Air Force. Another of the most popular and spectacular events in the royal ceremonial calendar has ended.

THE STATE OPENING OF PARLIAMENT

There is one occasion in the year when The Queen reads a speech which has been written for her by the Prime Minister of the day, and this is the speech she is required to read, word for word, with not a single syllable changed. The occasion is the State Opening of Parliament, on the day when Parliament assembles for the first time in the winter, and usually takes place in the first week of November. The Queen's speech outlines the proposed legislation to be introduced in the coming year by her Government and the event is a perfect example of a constitutional monarchy at work: a reigning sovereign carrying out the wishes of a democratically-elected government.

On the evening before the State Opening, the royal Regalia is brought from the Tower of London to the Palace. Brigadier Kenneth Mears, Deputy Governor of the Tower, has responsibility for the Crown Jewels and I asked him if there was a lot of red tape involved in moving the Regalia. I was surprised at his reply:

All that happens is that the Comptroller of the Lord Chamberlain's Office turns up at the Tower and signs a chit. I then hand over the Regalia, including the Imperial State Crown, and away it goes. After the ceremony at the Palace of Westminster the same procedure is carried out in reverse. It's as simple as that.

On the morning of the State Opening, the Regalia precedes the sovereign to Parliament, being carried in Queen Alexandra's State Coach which is lit from the inside so that spectators can clearly see the Imperial State Crown, the Cap of Maintenance, the Sword of State and the Maces of the Sergeants-at-Arms.

The Royal Procession from Buckingham Palace arrives at the Palace of Westminster at 11 a.m. The Queen, usually accompanied by the Duke of Edinburgh and Princess Anne or the Princess of Wales, travels in the Irish State Coach escorted by the Household Cavalry. Waiting to greet her are the Earl Marshal of England and the Lord Great Chamberlain, who is Hereditary Keeper of the Royal Palace of Westminster. The Lord Great Chamberlain is not to be confused with the Lord Chamberlain, Head of the Royal Household, who has to remain in Buckingham Palace when the sovereign is in Parliament as a 'hostage' for her safe return. When Lord Maclean was Lord Chamberlain he was always greeted by The Queen with the same words when she returned from the State Opening of Parliament: 'Have you minded the store well, Chips?' Chips being the nickname that everyone knew him by.

The Queen is then guided to the Robing Room, past a guard of honour of dismounted troopers carrying sabres. Inside the Robing Room her Ladies-in-Waiting dress Her Majesty in the Crimson Robe of State, made originally for Queen Victoria and whose 18-foot (5·5-m)-long train is carried by four Pages-of-Honour, usually the sons or grandsons of senior Members of the Household. The Imperial State Crown is placed on Her Majesty's head and when all is ready a fanfare is sounded, the doors to the Royal Gallery are opened and the Royal Procession moves towards the Chamber of the House of Lords. The proceedings have been televised live by the BBC since 1958, and members of the public are permitted to sit in the Royal Gallery to view the processions, although tickets are normally given on a 'first come first served' basis to the friends of peers and peeresses. Gentlemen are required to wear formal morning coats or uniform and ladies should wear gloves and hats.

Inside the Chamber of the House of Lords, everyone present has dressed as befits this special ceremonial occasion. The peers in their parliamentary robes of scarlet trimmed with ermine; their wives in long evening gowns and wearing diamond tiaras; the Archbishops and Bishops in their ecclesiastical garments; judges complete with robes and wigs and members of the diplomatic corps wearing every decoration in the book.

The reason the ceremony of the State Opening of Parliament takes place in the House of Lords is that the sovereign has no physical connection at all with the House of Commons. No Monarch has been allowed to enter the Commons since the days of Charles I and in order to hear The Queen's speech, Members of Parliament are summoned by Black Rod who marches in procession from the House of Lords. As he approaches the entrance to the Commons, clad in his uniform of black frock coat, lace collar, silk stockings and buckled shoes, the door is symbolically slammed in his face and not opened until he has knocked three times with his staff of office. He then delivers the message from The Queen 'commanding this Honourable House to attend her immediately in the House of Peers'.

The Speaker is first to leave the Commons, followed by the Prime Minister and the Leader of the Opposition and then Members of both sides. They walk slowly to the Lords where they are allowed only as far as the Bar of the House, which means that only very few of them can actually get inside and hear The Queen as she delivers the speech, which is afterwards debated in Parliament.

Once the speech has been read, Her Majesty returns to the Robing Room and is divested of the Imperial State Crown and the Royal Procession leaves for Buckingham Palace. The State Opening of Parliament is one of the shortest of all royal occasions, usually lasting just about an hour from start to finish.

THE GARTER SERVICE

The Most Noble Order of the Garter is the senior Order of Chivalry in the world, both in years and order of precedence. The story of its origin has been embroidered and retold throughout the centuries, with the most common theory being that, in 1348, King Edward III decided to form a body of élite knights who would swear personal allegiance to him. As St George was the patron saint of England, His Majesty wanted to take that name as the title of his new order. Legend has it that at a ball held after the victory at Calais in 1347, Joan, the Fair Maid of Kent, who was married at that time to the Earl of Salisbury, let her garter fall from her leg. This was an act usually associated with a woman of loose morals and all the courtiers present laughed at the poor woman's obvious discomfort.

Whereupon the King immediately retrieved the garter and tied it around his own leg uttering the immortal words: 'Honi Soit Qui Mal Y Pense', which is usually translated as: 'Evil be to him who evil thinks.' Whether it is true or not, it is a delightful story and the fact remains that the words were adopted as the motto of the Order of the Garter and the emblem of the Order is a dark blue velvet garter edged with gold.

The 'élitist' element of the Order of the Garter is maintained by the fact that its numbers are restricted to twenty-four plus the Royal Knights: the Duke of Edinburgh, who was installed by King George VI in 1947 shortly after installing the then Princess Elizabeth (because the King wanted to preserve her seniority), and Prince Charles, installed by his mother in 1958, the year he was named as Prince of Wales.

There is also a number of 'Extra Knights', a category introduced to honour foreign royalty. These are: the King of Norway (1959); the King of the Belgians (1963); the Emperor of Japan (whose name was reinstated in 1971 after it had been struck off in 1941 on the orders of King George VI); the Grand Duke of Luxembourg (1972) and the King of Sweden (1983). In 1910, King Edward VI decided to revive the practice of appointing Ladies of the Garter. Queen Elizabeth the Queen Mother was appointed in 1936 and there are two Extra Ladies of the Garter, Queen Juliana of the Netherlands (1958) and the Queen of Denmark (1979). Her Majesty The Queen is Sovereign of the Order as she is of all nine Orders of Chivalry in Britain.

Attached to the Order of the Garter are the thirteen Military Knights of Windsor, who were formed at the same time in 1348. Originally called the Poor Knights, they came into being after the wars in France when many of them had been prisoners; they lost all their money after ransoms for their release had been paid. They were given small pensions and quarters at Windsor Castle, for which they were required to be in attendance at morning service in St George's Chapel as representatives of the Knights of the Garter. It was in 1833 that King William IV changed their designation to the Military Knights and granted them their present uniform, which consists of a scarlet tail coat with white cross sword belt, crimson sash and cocked hat with plume. These days the Military Knights are all retired army officers (who would have applied to the Military Secretary at the Army Department of the Ministry of Defence) and live in houses just inside King Henry VIII's Gate, the main entrance to Windsor Castle.

The Garter Service takes place on a Monday in June, when members of the public are allowed to witness the procession which leads from the Castle to St George's Chapel. Tickets are free but you have to apply to the Lord Chamberlain's Office in St James's Palace before the end of February to stand a chance of obtaining one. Sir Cenydd Traherne has been a Knight of the Garter since 1970 and he describes what the day is like, viewed from the inside:

We arrive at Windsor Castle around eleven and I go off to the room where I put on my robes, mantle and collar. Then all the Knights move to the Throne Room, if there is an investiture taking place. These all happen in private and they really are the most magnificent occasions. The Queen fastens the garter just below your left knee, then the mantle and the ribbon of the Order is attached, with The Queen assisting in all these acts. Each new Knight has two sponsors who show him what to do and where to stand. There is a tremendous sense of occasion, which is enhanced by the presence of the Yeomen of the Guard, The Queen's Bodyguard, who stand around the walls, and of course the other members of the Royal Family who are in attendance. Then the Prelate of the Order administers the Oath and there is a short service. Once these formalities have been observed you return to the Robing Room and leave your cloak, before a short reception with the Royal Family before lunch. This is a delightful interlude because your wife is invited and the whole thing is completely informal. Lunch is held in the Waterloo Chamber and it is truly a magnificent affair – with no speeches. At half past two you go back to the Robing Room to get ready for the march down to St George's Chapel. First there are the Military Knights of Windsor, followed by the Heralds and Pursuivants. Then we, the members of the Order, walk in front of the Queen Mother and the royal princes and finally The Queen's Procession which includes the Duke of Edinburgh, with the Yeomen of the Guard bringing up the rear.

The crowds are very close and we can always hear what they are saying, which is sometimes quite amusing. Of course there are the two guards bands playing along the route and the troopers of the Household Cavalry to add to the ceremonial, so it really is a very colourful scene. Inside St George's Chapel each Knight has his personal stall with his crest over it and we have a short and very simple service which lasts only for about half an hour. Then The Queen and the royal party leave by carriage and the rest of us are driven by car back to the Castle. The ceremony is the same year after year but each time I find something new and I wouldn't miss it for the world.

ROYAL GARDEN PARTIES

Every year The Queen holds four Garden Parties, or to give them their official title, Afternoon Parties. Three are held in the grounds of Buckingham Palace and one in the garden of the Palace of Holyrood-house in Edinburgh. They take place in early July and some 9000 people are invited to each one, with 4000 invited to the one in Scotland.

The Garden Parties provide a democratic way for the monarch to meet a large number of her subjects and other guests, and they have replaced the old-style 'coming out' balls at which young débutantes – ladies of high birth, or at least those whose fathers had plenty of money – were presented at Court. The organisation of the Garden Parties is the responsibility of the Lord Chamberlain's Office in St James's Palace (see page 44). It is usual for between 8000 and 9000 guests to turn up at Buckingham Palace for each party. These range from the council worker who has been invited as a reward for long service to his community, to the Archbishops, diplomats and senior politicians who receive invitations every year. The

94

name of every person who has ever been invited to a Garden Party is retained in a card index system, together with information such as the number of times they have attended; if they have refused an invitation; and also if their children have accompanied them: unmarried daughters aged eighteen and over are allowed to accompany their parents – sons are not! The first indication one has is when a large white envelope pops through the letterbox. It is usually addressed to the lady of the house and is unstamped. There is simply a cypher containing the legend EIIR in the lower left-hand corner. The stiff paste-board card inside says:

The Lord Chamberlain is commanded by Her Majesty
to invite (the names follow)
to a Garden Party at Buckingham Palace on
(the appropriate date) from 4 to 6 p.m.

In the lower left-hand corner are the words: Morning Dress, Uniform or Lounge suit. It was at The Queen's personal insistence that this last point was included. When the guest lists were extended to include people from all walks of life, Her Majesty was anxious that no one should be excluded because they could not afford a morning suit, so she decided that lounge suits would be perfectly acceptable. Nevertheless, they are the exception, and the majority of male guests wear formal morning clothes complete with top hat. Ladies always wear hats and trouser suits are definitely frowned upon. Together with the invitation is a map showing the three entrances to Buckingham Palace, which points out the nearest underground railway stations. Those guests who wish to drive to the Palace are given a special car pass to place inside the windscreen so that on the day in question the police can identify their vehicle and allow them to park in one of the approach roads. Most of the guests opt for the Grand Entrance because this gives them the opportunity of actually going inside Buckingham Palace itself; for many of them it may be the only occasion when they will be able to do so. The other two entrances open directly onto the garden itself. The queues start forming shortly after lunch and at 3.15 p.m. the gates are opened. After crossing the forecourt one enters the Grand Entrance and ascends the Main Staircase with its rich red carpet before passing into the Bow Room, having first delivered up any cameras to the courteous but firm attendants who politely inform you that photography of any sort is strictly forbidden at Garden Parties. A lot of people try to linger as long as possible in the Bow Room to see at least a fraction of the treasures contained in the Palace.

The gardens are spread over forty acres (16 ha) with a lake at the west end containing a flock of pink flamingos. The tea tents are arranged along the southern wall and old hands usually head for their refreshments

95

as soon as they arrive. They know the newcomers will probably wait to see The Queen first and then there is always a crush at the last minute. Several varieties of tea are available, but the most popular drink is iced coffee. Cakes, sticky buns and gateaux are served, but no alcohol. At precisely 4 p.m. The Queen, attended by several other members of the Royal Family, appears through the glass doors of the Bow Room and stands at the top of the Garden Steps as one of the two military bands on duty plays the national anthem. Any guests who are still arriving at this time are locked inside the Palace until The Queen has passed. The Royal Family then splits up and each takes one of the 'lanes' in which the guests are arranged. A group of distinguished-looking gentlemen, all very tall, with the unmistakable air of former officers in the Brigade of Guards, have marshalled the guests and gone through the preliminary task of sorting out who is to be 'presented'. This has nothing whatever to do with the rank of the person concerned; if someone is wearing an unusual uniform, a particular decoration or perhaps is handicapped, they may have something interesting to tell The Queen so they stand a reasonable chance of being selected.

As Her Majesty walks slowly through the lanes acknowledging the applause of her guests, one of the Gentlemen Ushers will murmur in her ear that, for instance, 'The gentleman you are about to meet, Ma'am, has been a dustman for nearly fifty years and never missed a day's work.' To the astonishment of the guest, The Queen will offer her hand and remark how pleased she is to meet someone with such a remarkable work record.

Meanwhile other members of the Family will be 'working' their lanes in the same way and somehow they discreetly coordinate it so that they all arrive at the tea tent at the same time. If someone gets a bit nervous or tends to talk for too long, royalty seems to have a knack of moving on without giving offence. The distance they have travelled is no more than 300 yards (274 m) but it will have taken over an hour to walk it. The royal tea tent is protected by more ushers and you have to have a special invitation to enter. This is where the diplomatic guests take their refreshments and outside, a line of chairs has been arranged in a semi-circle, so that a number of ladies, who have already laid claim to the seats, can watch, from a respectful distance, the royal party taking their tea. At 5.50 p.m. precisely, The Queen will leave the royal marquee and walk slowly (she never hurries) back towards the Palace. The guests, somewhat reluctantly, start to go home, taking as long as possible over their departure. For another year a Garden Party is over.

THE ROYAL MAUNDY

On Maundy Thursday, 27 March 1986, The Queen distributed 120 bags,

Previous page: the Sovereign's Birthday Parade: as The Queen passes the Horse Guards Building, she salutes her mother, who watches from a room above the archway; *above:* the Queen Mother playing pool during a visit to a Youth Centre in Jersey; *right:* Princess Anne with Zara and Peter Phillips, watching the Windsor Horse Show; *opposite above:* the Queen Mother with a personal detective and one of the famous corgis, enjoying a stroll on a Norfolk beach; *opposite below:* The Queen and the Amir of Bahrain during the Royal tour of the Gulf States

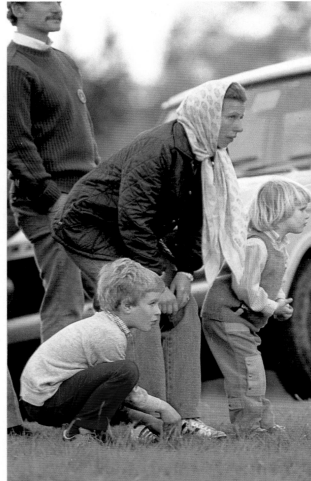

Opposite page: the Duke of Edinburgh visiting Nepal in his capacity as President of the World Wildlife Fund; *above:* Sarah Ferguson and Prince Andrew watch a polo match on Smith's Lawn, Windsor, shortly before their wedding day; *left:* the Princess of Wales enjoying an enthusiastic reception in Victoria, Australia

Above: a gallant gesture from the Prince of Wales after his mother The Queen has presented him with his victory trophy at the Windsor Polo Ground; *left:* the Prince and Princess of Wales expressing affection in public to a degree which would have been thought impossible in previous generations; *opposite above:* the Prince of Wales relaxes after a tough polo match at Cirencester; *opposite below:* a portrait of Prince Edward taken on his eighteenth birthday while he was a student at Cambridge; *overleaf:* the Princess of Wales leads Prince William and Prince Harry down the steps of one of The Queen's Flight aircraft

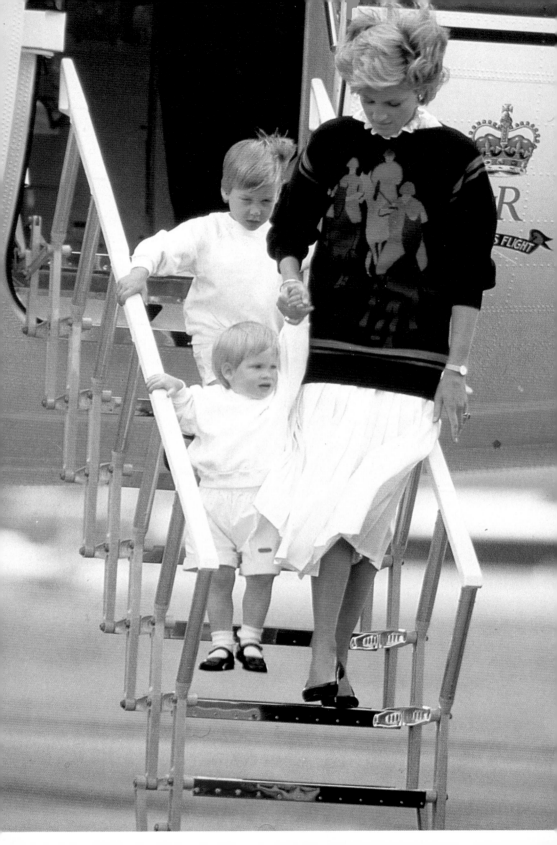

each containing twenty-four coins, to sixty men and sixty women in Chichester Cathedral. The coins were specially minted for the occasion and they were contained in a white purse with red strings. This was The Royal Maundy, a royal ceremony as old as the monarchy itself.

Every year, on the day before Good Friday, the sovereign gives to members of the 'well-deserving poor' as many coins as she has years, plus one for 'the year of Grace', to an equal number of recipients. The coins, which of course are worth far more than their intrinsic value, are silver pennies to the value of one, two, three and four sterlings – the name of the original penny weight in Norman times. It is from this ancient weight that we get the description of 'pound sterling' today. Although the custom has been followed by every British sovereign, there was a period in the Middle Ages when the kings and queens themselves did not take part personally but sent high-ranking members of their households to distribute the gifts. The reason for this was that in those days, the poor were also usually the diseased and unwashed, and even though the sovereigns wished to continue an age-old practice, they did not feel that democracy should extend as far as washing the feet of the poor, which was part of the original ceremony. This part of the Maundy Service has been discontinued since the end of the seventeenth century, but one symbolic link has remained. The Queen is still presented with sweet-smelling nosegays by children of the parish, as a reminder of those far-off days when the odours of the poor were considered a little too strong for the delicate sensibilities of royalty.

The Maundy Service usually takes place in Westminster Abbey and every other year at a cathedral outside London; this was an innovation initiated by The Queen herself. Prior to her reign it was always held in Westminster Abbey and in fact the Royal Maundy was the first public duty she attended after her coronation in June 1953. It is a comparatively short and simple ceremony, lasting just over three-quarters of an hour, but impressive none the less with The Queen's Bodyguard of the Yeomen of the Guard on duty in their full ceremonial uniforms.

The Senior Yeoman has the task of carrying the dish containing the alms to be distributed. It's a singular honour to be chosen but one which becomes more onerous as the years go by. The older The Queen gets, the more money is placed in the dish and the heavier it is to carry, so the Yeoman goes into weight training for some weeks before Maundy Thursday to get fit.

Those who receive the Royal Maundy are chosen on the recommendation of the clergy of the diocese to be visited. They have to be over sixty-five, are usually not very well off and are presented with the Maundy Money as a reward for years of Christian service. It's a completely ecumenical choice, with members of other churches, Roman Catholic, Free Church and Salvation Army, joining those who belong to the established Church of England.

The men and women who are to receive the Royal Maundy sit on opposite sides of the church. The Queen goes down one side handing out purses to the women first, then back up the opposite side, repeating the ceremony for the men. The value of the coins being distributed is not very much these days, but the fact that they have been given personally by The Queen makes them unique gifts and very few recipients are ever persuaded to part with them.

REMEMBRANCE SUNDAY

The Remembrance Day ceremony and parade in which The Queen takes part every November is one of the most moving and emotional occasions of the year. The Cenotaph in Whitehall is the focal point of the ceremony, erected to commemorate 'The Glorious Dead' of two World Wars.

The Prime Minister, the Leader of the Opposition, Cabinet Ministers and politicians of every party assemble before the war memorial, and The Queen, accompanied by the Princes of the Blood and the Royal Dukes, stands in silent tribute as the clock strikes eleven. Then Her Majesty places her own wreath of poppies on the Cenotaph, followed by those of the other male members of the Royal Family. The ladies watch from a window overlooking Whitehall. A short service is conducted by the Bishop of London who is also Dean of the Chapels Royal and then comes the march past by the men and women of Britain and the Commonwealth. Soldiers, past and present, many wearing medals won for gallantry in campaigns long forgotten, march proudly to the tunes they remember from years ago. The Cenotaph gradually fills with wreaths and floral tributes as the seemingly never-ending procession winds its way past. The Remembrance Day Parade is seen on television every year and is considered to be an anchronism by some these days. But The Queen insists on being present and from the number of people who turn up to watch and take part in the parade, its popularity – if that is the right word – is in no danger of diminishing.

THE ROYAL CALENDAR

These then are the main royal occasions which take place year in, year out. In addition there are the annual ceremonial events which do not receive quite the same amount of attention from the public but which are still important events in the royal calendar.

The Sovereign's Parade at Sandhurst This celebrates the annual Passing Out of officer cadets at the Royal Military Academy towards the end of

July. The highlight of the ceremony is at the end of the parade when the Adjutant of the College traditionally rides his horse up the steps of the Grand Entrance and into the building itself.

The Chelsea Flower Show Every May the gardens of the Royal Hospital on the Chelsea Embankment, home of the famous Chelsea Pensioners, are transformed into a floral wonderland by gardeners from all over the world. On the evening before the show opens, The Queen and other members of the Royal Family pay a private visit.

The Royal Film Performance, the Royal Variety Show and the Royal Command Performance Every year the entertainment industry puts on a number of performances on stage and film, which have been chosen to be honoured by The Queen's presence. Tickets are sold at highly inflated prices with the proceeds being donated to charity. The film selected for a Royal Performance is discussed with the Private Secretary who will then talk to The Queen to see if it is regarded as 'suitable'. Similarly the material used by comedians and singers at a Royal Variety Show is vetted, but reference to members of the Royal Family in the script is not vetoed. These occasions give members of the public a chance to see The Queen in evening dress and wearing some of the diamonds and jewels from the royal collection.

Royal Ascot Another opportunity for more people to see The Queen and her Family at close quarters comes at the Royal Ascot Race Meeting held in June. Her Majesty hosts a large house party at Windsor Castle and every afternoon before the day's racing begins, she and her guests drive down the famous Long Walk to the racecourse, where they transfer into the State carriages for the Royal Procession up the course before the grandstands. This is not a State occasion, but it is one of the most popular of royal events and coincides with the Garter Service which is held on the Monday of Royal Ascot Week.

For many of those attending Royal Ascot it is the social event of the year. Gentlemen wear formal morning clothes and the ladies' dresses are the focus of attention for television cameras and photographers. Each year the fashions seem to become more outrageous and one regular visitor to the Royal Enclosure, Mrs Gertrude Shilling, is renowned for the startling hats she wears, each one more daring and flamboyant than the last. Her Majesty's Representative at Ascot, who has an office in St James's Palace, issues vouchers to the Royal Enclosure and guidelines on the correct dress. Convicted felons are prohibited and, until recently, divorced men and women were also refused entry. Ladies are advised to wear hats, and trouser suits are absolutely forbidden.

Changing of the Guard Of course the most frequent piece of royal ceremonial is the Changing of the Guard at Buckingham Palace. This takes place every morning during the summer months, and every other morning in the winter. It happens at 11.30 a.m. and is one of London's biggest tourist attractions – and it's free!

Visitors who turn up outside the railings sometimes ask if The Queen is 'at home'. It is easy to tell because if she is, the royal Standard will be flying: if she is not in residence the flag is not flown. There is also a significant difference in the size of the guard when Her Majesty is at the Palace. Three officers and forty other ranks are on parade when she is 'at home' and three officers and thirty-one other ranks when she is away.

There is also daily 'guard mounting'. This takes place at: St James's Palace, still the senior of the royal palaces; at the Tower of London, even though it has not been used as a royal residence for more than 200 years; at Windsor Castle and at Horse Guards Arch in Whitehall, which is the only place where the cavalry perform the duty. This is because Horse Guards Arch was originally the entrance to St James's Palace and custom dictates that the senior regiment in the Royal Guard should retain the honour of guarding this oldest of royal doorways. Horse Guards Arch is the most exclusive thoroughfare in England. Only those of royal blood are allowed to use it and one of the few occasions when The Queen drives through it is en route to Westminster for the State Opening of Parliament.

One important part of the sovereign's role and one which involves a great deal of ceremonial is when she acts as host to a foreign Head of State. There are usually three State Visits every year and each one requires about three months' preparation. Invitations are never extended until it is known they will be accepted, so the negotiations are conducted in advance by the Foreign Office in conjunction with the Cabinet Office and the Royal Household. A State Visit is an important act of diplomacy in modern terms and has a purpose far beyond merely entertaining another Head of State.

ROYAL TRANSPORT

Because of the vast amount of travelling The Queen does every year, it follows that her various modes of transport, and the ways in which she uses them, have become a vitally important part of her working life.

There are three main departments dealing with the travel requirements of the Royal Family: The Queen's Flight, which has responsibility whenever and wherever a member of the Family is travelling by air (even if he or she is not using one of the Flight's own aircraft); the Crown Equerry's department at the Royal Mews, which looks after all transport by road, whether it's by royal limousine, private car, on horseback or in one of the State carriages used on formal occasions; and the Royal Yacht *Britannia*, which is an independent command within the Royal Navy and the only ship whose Captain is also an Admiral. In addition there is the Royal Train which is administered by British Rail and for which The Queen pays whenever she needs it.

THE QUEEN'S FLIGHT

A great deal of use is made of air transport: The Queen's Flight, based at RAF Benson in Oxfordshire, flies more than 800 operations a year, both at home and overseas. Formed originally by King Edward VIII in July 1936 as The King's Flight, it consisted in those days of a single aircraft and the King's personal pilot Flt. Lt. Edward Fielden, who was to become Air Commodore Sir Edward Fielden, KCVO, CB, DFC, AFC.

Edward VIII is credited as being the first member of the Royal Family to fly, when (as Prince of Wales) he travelled as a passenger to the Italian front in 1918, during the last year of the First World War. However, his father King George V distrusted air travel and forbade his children to fly for many years.

Today, The Queen's Flight has a total of 180 personnel, with only two women – both civilians. The fleet of five aircraft – three Andovers and two Westland Wessex helicopters – has just been supplemented with two BAe 146 medium range jet aircraft, bringing The Queen's Flight into the jet age for the first time.

The Flight is manned by a Captain, currently Air Vice-Marshal John de Severne, MVO, OBE, AFC, two Deputy Captains and seven crews. The Captain is also a member of the Royal Household and he accompanies

101

both The Queen and Queen Elizabeth the Queen Mother whenever they travel by air. The Queen's Flight comes under the direct control of Her Majesty herself. She sees every request for an aircraft and she has been known to refuse members of her family if she thinks the reason is perhaps slightly frivolous. So there is no question these days of anyone asking for an aircraft of The Queen's Flight just to go racing or on any other purely social engagement. There is also a strict 'pecking order' for those who are permitted to use the Flight and it follows the order of precedence in the Royal Family. So if, for example, one of the junior members has booked an aircraft for a particular day and then the Duke of Edinburgh decides he needs the aircraft on that same day, there is no question about who gives way.

Those permitted to use The Queen's Flight, always with the written permission of The Queen, are members of her family, senior government ministers and certain service chiefs. The system is that if someone wants to travel by air, the Private Secretary will telephone the secretary of The Queen's Flight at Benson and make the request – usually several weeks, sometimes months in advance. The secretary then writes to The Queen's Private Secretary, Sir William Heseltine, who will place the request before Her Majesty. Once The Queen is satisfied that there is a valid reason for the flight, permission is granted and the proposed flight is entered into the official diary – the 'bible' by which The Queen's Flight lives. A short time before the journey is to take place a reconnaissance flight will be undertaken over the route to check things like landing conditions, security and times of arrival. This does not always happen in the United Kingdom, where the crews are usually familiar with the routes to be flown, but always when there is an overseas flight in prospect. If The Queen is to make one of her frequent visits to a foreign country and is travelling by air, the Captain himself will look after the 'recce'; otherwise one of his Deputy Captains goes along.

The day before a royal flight, the crew will assemble to check that everything is in order. The Queen's Steward, an RAF sergeant, will see that the royal compartment in the aircraft is exactly as that day's particular passenger likes it. The Queen, for example, likes to sit in the rear seat on the left-hand side of the aircraft; the Duke of Kent doesn't mind sitting with his 'back to the engine', and the Duke of Edinburgh and the Prince of Wales frequently take the controls. Both the latter are qualified pilots who were taught to fly by The Queen's Flight and they can both handle fixed-wing aircraft and helicopters. But they are never allowed to captain any aircraft they fly. Technically they are still 'under training', even though they sit in the 'left-hand' or captain's seat when they are flying. The Steward then checks the menu for the day. Food on royal flights is usually plain but good – the crew reckon it is about on a par with the fare served to first-class passengers on a commercial airline.

The Andovers are the aircraft used most frequently in this country and even though they are more then twenty-five years old they are in magnificent condition. Inside they are functional rather than luxurious with three separate compartments. The front is for the servicing crew who always accompany the aircraft: The Queen's Flight does all its own maintenance, at home and abroad. Then there is a middle compartment for members of the Royal Household: eight seats, four each side, set in pairs facing each other across small tables. Beyond this compartment is the royal cabin, containing four large armchair-like seats. The decor is in subtle shades of blue and grey and as there is no public address system on board, the royal passengers communicate with the pilot by way of written notes passed by the steward. At the rear of the aircraft is a small toilet with a selection of perfumes and soaps. The members of The Queen's Flight who come into the most frequent contact with the Royal Family say their royal passengers want to be treated with the minimum of fuss. For all flights within Britain a 'purple airway' is designated whenever a member of the Royal Family is flying. This is a corridor ten miles (16 km) wide and stretching for 1000 feet (305 m) above and below the royal aircraft. Unless under strict air traffic control, no other aircraft is allowed within that airspace and the 'purple airway' lasts from fifteen minutes before a royal flight takes off until fifteen minutes after it has landed.

The royal aircraft are quite distinctive and easily recognisable. The upper part of the fuselage is painted bright red, while the lower half is highly polished silver, with blue and white trim. The helicopters are also bright red and are frequently seen over London as they land and take off from the gardens behind Buckingham Palace. In recent years the most frequent passenger with The Queen's Flight has been Princess Anne, followed by the Duke of Edinburgh, the Prince of Wales and the Duke of Gloucester. Queen Elizabeth the Queen Mother uses the helicopters as often as any of the other ladies and has been known to describe them as 'my version of the London bus'. The Queen rarely travels by helicopter; in fact there are only two recorded flights during her reign. These were in August 1977 – Jubilee Year – on a visit to Northern Ireland, when for security reasons it was felt necessary to use a helicopter, and again in 1984, when Her Majesty attended the fortieth anniversary celebrations of the D-Day landings in Normandy. The rules governing members of the Royal Family flying together have been laid down for safety reasons. The Queen and the Prince of Wales (heir to the throne) do not fly in the same aircraft, but the Prince and his own children do fly together, a decision taken only after long discussions within the Royal

Family. There are no restrictions on other members of the family flying in the same aircraft.

Whenever a royal passenger is on board one of the aircraft, their personal standard is flown as soon as they touch down. There is a small store located in The Queen's Flight hangar at Benson containing more than 600 flags. They claim to have one for every country in the world and certain members of the Royal Family have a number of different standards which have to be displayed. For example when the Prince of Wales is in Wales he flies a different standard from the one he uses in Scotland, where his title is Duke of Rothesay, and there is yet another one to be used when he is acting as Duke of Cornwall. One of the most delicate problems arises when a member of the Royal Family represents The Queen at an independence ceremony in one of Britain's former colonies. The Union Flag is flown when they arrive in the country and the new standard has to be displayed the moment independence has been declared. So it means a constant updating for the flag store – so far they have never been caught out!

Among the many items the stores have been asked to provide are overhead hammocks for the children of the Prince and Princess of Wales when they were babies. One of the biggest problems with the Andovers is the fact that they do not have baggage holds, so all the royal luggage has to be stored inside the aircraft. As most members of the Royal Family travel with large wardrobes – especially on an extended overseas tour – it can cause problems for the stewards on board. Also the Andovers are restricted to flying below 20,000 feet (6096 m), and this has occasionally meant flying in bad weather through icy and turbulent conditions. All this will now change with the introduction of the BAe 146 jets. They are much larger than the Andovers and have proper baggage holds, so the comfort of the royal passengers and the crews will be greatly increased. And of course, the jets can fly above the clouds at speeds nearly twice as fast as the turbo prop Andovers, so there will be an enormous saving in time.

At the moment, the cost of running The Queen's Flight is around £5 million a year. It has been estimated that to abolish the Flight and use commercial airlines for the same amount of travel would increase the costs by thirty per cent.

The Queen's Flight has an enviable safety record. There has never been a serious accident and they have never lost a passenger. Security is an important factor and for this reason many of the airmen who volunteer to serve in the Flight remain for many years. The Royal Family like to see the same faces around them year after year, and as this is the only 'airline' in the world which does not issue tickets, the crews need to be able to recognise who their passengers are. Obviously this doesn't apply to the immediate members of the Royal Family, but it does to the other people who use the Flight.

The men who fly The Queen and her Family are all volunteers and they represent the cream of the Royal Air Force's talent. As an example of the calibre of the aircrew who have served in The Queen's Flight it is worth noting that in 1948 (when it was still The King's Flight of course), the pilot of Workshop Aircraft Viking VL248 was Flight Lieutenant E. B. Trubshaw, who later went on to become one of the most famous airmen in the world as the test pilot of Concorde.

THE ROYAL TRAIN

The Queen and her immediate Family have the choice of some of the most privileged forms of transport: private aircraft; the Royal Yacht; horse-drawn carriages; luxury limousines. But when I recently asked Princess Anne what was her favourite way to travel, she replied without any hesitation: 'The Train'.

In her case, of course, it's not an InterCity 125 or a tiny branch line through the Cotswolds, but the Royal Train which today is the only private train service running in Britain. It is reminiscent of the old days of the great railway barons who used their private railway cars as travelling saloons – luxury on wheels. And though it isn't quite like that today, having briefly seen what life is like on board the Royal Train, I can fully understand why not only Princess Anne but most of the other members of the Royal Family prefer it to any of the other ways in which they are able to move around the world.

The Royal Train is in itself something of a misnomer. There is no such thing as *the* Royal Train. There is no one train which qualifies for this distinction. There are in fact thirteen vehicles which are specifically used to make up a Royal Train and it is possible to see two Royal Trains in different parts of the country on the same day.

The trains are maintained by British Rail and come under the responsibility of the Passenger Services Manager, Mr Terry Worrall, who says that the inside of the Royal Compartments today do not in any way compare with earlier Royal Trains such as those on display at the National Railway Museum in York. In fact Mr Worrall claims the furnishings in the present day Royal Trains are 'positively spartan in comparison with those used in Victorian times'. Well I think spartan is a little extreme to describe what I feel are very comfortable quarters. True they are not luxurious, but neither is there any doubt about the comfort and style of the way the Royal Family travel by rail. If The Queen and the Duke of Edinburgh are travelling together, there will be ten vehicles formed into one train. This is the largest single Royal Train and includes

Her Majesty's Personal Saloon, His Royal Highness's Personal Saloon, a sitting room, bathrooms, bedrooms and offices for the Household and staff, accommodation for the railway staff and, somewhat surprisingly, 'Traveller's Fare', the catering service provided by British Rail.

The Queen's personal quarters are decorated in light pastel shades of beige and in her saloon, which is the full width of the vehicle, there are easy chairs, and a sofa upholstered in pale blue with handstitched velvet cushions and a small coffee table. The paintings on the walls recall a more glamorous age in the history of royal trains. Adjoining is the bedroom and bathroom.

The Duke of Edinburgh's apartments reflect his own tastes with a simple dining room capable of seating up to ten people for a meal, in which he frequently holds working meetings. The colour scheme is plain brown and the armchairs discourage one from staying too long. There is no corridor through the royal apartments, so Members of the Household do not move through it unless they have a specific reason for doing so. Many of the journeys involve overnight travel, so there's an informal, hotel-like atmosphere about the train which is the main reason why the Royal Family enjoy it so much. They can relax on board secure in the knowledge that they are surrounded by trusted friends and staff.

The plans for each of the royal journeys are forwarded to British Rail Headquarters twice a year and then the individual requirements are dealt with at the five regional offices of the service. I was slightly surprised to discover that there is no special driver for the Royal Train. With The Queen having a personal pilot and an Admiral as Captain of the Royal Yacht, it might seem logical that there would also be someone designated to drive the Royal Train, but apparently this is not the case. According to Terry Worrall it is purely taken in turn on the respective roster of the depot concerned. Obviously there are depots which have provided drivers on a number of occasions, so it isn't quite as haphazard as it sounds, but there is no single specific individual at any one location whose task is to drive the Royal Train. However, British Rail do tend to allocate the same stewards to work on the Royal Trains. The Royal Family is known to like seeing familiar faces around them and as long as it fits in with the commitments of the catering service, the same staff generally work for the same member of the Family.

The outside of the carriages which make up the Royal Train are painted in a distinctive shade of claret and because they do not always stop at railway stations – overnight stops are invariably at out-of-the-way sidings – they carry their own set of steps and boarding platform. The rolling stock of the present Royal Train is now more than thirty years old; some of it as much as fifty years old. So in 1986 a brand-new Royal Train was delivered at a cost of £7 million. It meant that they were able to keep up with the rest of British Rail's high-speed trains which are capable of speeds of more than 100 miles an hour. The previous train was restricted to below seventy miles an hour, both for safety and for the comfort of the royal passengers. In an age when jet travel is taken for granted and a journey across the world can be undertaken in a matter of hours, it is refreshing to know that for The Queen and her Family, there is still a great deal of pleasure in being able to see the countryside and travel in the same way as Queen Victoria did – even if it's not quite the age of steam!

THE ROYAL MEWS

Whenever The Queen travels by road, whether by carriage, on horseback or by motor car, she becomes the responsibility of the Crown Equerry, Lt.-Col. Sir John Miller, the man who runs the Royal Mews. Sir John lives in an imposing 'Grace and Favour' house just inside the entrance to the Royal Mews in Buckingham Palace Road, and every morning he can be seen making his rounds, checking the horses and the staff, whose days are dedicated to making sure that The Queen and her Family always arrive safely and on time.

The titular head of the Royal Mews is actually the Master of the Horse, who ranks third in order of precedence at Court, behind the Lord Great Chamberlain and the Lord Steward. But these days his duties are mainly ceremonial: he can be seen riding immediately behind the sovereign in State processions.

Of the five Rolls-Royce limousines in the Royal Mews, the most important is the Phantom VI given to Her Majesty in March 1978; a gift to mark the Silver Jubilee from the Society of Motor Manufacturers and Traders. This car, in common with the other two most recent models, is equipped with a removable outer roof covering, which leaves a transparent inner lining made of plastic. This is used to enable onlookers to have a clear view of the royal passengers both during the day and at night, when the interior of the car is illuminated by fluorescent strip lighting. The five Rolls-Royces are State limousines and as such carry no registration number plates. They are all painted in the royal maroon livery and are fitted with special brackets to hold the shields bearing the royal coat of arms and the personal pennants of the royal passengers. The oldest car in royal service is a Phantom IV built in 1948, with a body by Mulliner. This car has been in continuous use for nearly forty years and is still in immaculate condition. The year following the coronation saw the introduction of a Rolls-Royce landaulette, which is the car frequently used when The Queen and the Duke of Edinburgh are abroad. There is a special place in the hold of *Britannia* for the car and it has been seen in every Commonwealth country. The other two Rolls-Royces are Phantom Vs and these were delivered in 1960 and 1961. There are also two Austin Princess limousines which are used by members of the Royal Family for official duties, and it was while she was travelling in one of these that an attempt was made to kidnap Princess Anne in The Mall in March, 1974 (see page 46).

Whenever The Queen is travelling in one of her official cars a solid silver mascot depicting St George and the Dragon is transferred to the bonnet. It was specially designed for her when she was Princess Elizabeth and was originally made out of spun sugar as the centrepiece for her wedding cake.

The Royal Family's private vehicles are also kept in the garages of the Royal Mews. The Queen favours a Rover saloon and a Vauxhall estate car of doubtful vintage, while the Duke of Edinburgh has a Range Rover plus a 15-cwt (762-kg) van which is powered by electric batteries and which was a gift from the makers. Prince Edward has a 135-m.p.h. (217-kph) Rover Vitesse, while the Duke of York, when he is on leave from the navy, drives a Jaguar, which is also Prince Charles's current car – in addition to a Range Rover and an Aston Martin. Princess Anne has remained loyal to Reliant: she drives a Scimitar GTE with a fibreglass body and a 2·8-litre engine, while the Princess of Wales uses a high-performance Ford Escort.

The Royal Mews at Buckingham Palace dates from 1825 and the present handsome quarters were designed by John Nash on the orders of George IV. They are still largely unchanged from Nash's original concept, which is in itself a tribute to his foresight and skill. The Mews (the word comes from an old French word describing a change of coat or feathers, and was the medieval place where the king's falcons would be housed during their 'mewing' or change of coat) is constructed around a quadrangle with the east side reserved for the State coaches and carriages and the horses stabled on the north and west sides. Above the coach houses is a number of flats where members of the Mews staff live, rent free. The historic State coaches are all kept in immaculate condition. The most fabulous of them all is undoubtedly the *Gold State Coach* which has been employed at every coronation since that of George IV, and which was also used to convey The Queen and the Duke of Edinburgh to St Paul's Cathedral for the Thanksgiving Service during Her Majesty's Silver Jubilee year in 1977. It was the first time the four-ton coach had been to St Paul's and the Crown Equerry had to carry out test runs before the event to make sure the eight greys (who pull it at no more than walking pace) could cope with the incline of Ludgate Hill. The Gold State Coach was built in 1762 for George III, who used it the day after taking delivery to attend the Opening of Parliament. It is 24 feet (7.3 m) long, 8 feet 3 inches (2.5 m) wide and 12 feet (3.7 m) high. The body consists of eight palm trees which support the roof, with the four corner trees loaded with trophies symbolising British victories in the Seven Years War. On the roof are three cherubs representing England, Scotland and Ireland. They support the Royal Crown and hold in their hands the Sceptre, Sword of State and the Ensign of Knighthood. The coach is gilded all over and covered with panels painted by Giovanni Battista Cipriani, one of Florence's most successful historical painters of the eighteenth century. The harness is of rich red morocco leather and the coachman's footboard is in the shape of a large scallop shell.

When The Queen goes to the State Opening of Parliament in November she invariably travels in the *Irish State Coach*, so named because the man who built it was at that time also Lord Mayor of Dublin. It was designed for Queen Victoria who bought it in 1852, but the original was destroyed by fire in 1911 and the present Irish State Coach is an identical copy. It is much lighter, in weight and appearance, than the Gold State Coach and its panels are painted black, adorned in gold with the royal coat of arms and the insignia of the Order of the Garter. There are brass lamps at each corner and on the roof the Royal Crown is supported by an intricate network of gilt-covered metalwork. (In fact, the only occasion when one of the State carriages has not been used to carry the sovereign to the State Opening of Parliament was in 1936, during the brief reign of Edward VIII. The weather was so bad on the day in question that the King decided to use a closed motor car, much to the disappointment of the watching crowd. As he had never been crowned, he was also unable to wear the Imperial State Crown which tradition demands, so he wore instead the cocked hat of an Admiral of the Fleet.)

The *Scottish State Coach* is third in importance in the Royal Mews. The crown of Scotland is mounted on its roof and the sides carry the royal arms of Scotland and the insignia of the Order of the Thistle, Scotland's premier order of chivalry. Naturally, The Queen uses this coach for all State occasions in Scotland but it has also been used many times in London. Queen Elizabeth the Queen Mother travelled in it during the Silver Jubilee celebrations and she is known to regard this coach with particular favour. Of all three major State coaches this is by far the most comfortable to ride in. It is regarded as the most elegant and because of the glass panels in its roof and large windows the light inside is superb. The coach originates from 1830, but was completely refurbished by an Edinburgh company in 1969.

The wedding of the Prince and Princess of Wales was the most televised event the world had then seen, watched by more than 500 million people throughout the world. After the ceremony the happy couple left for the return to Buckingham Palace in the *1902 State Landau*, which Prince Charles and his brother Prince Andrew had used for the drive to St Paul's. The 1902 State Landau is an open carriage and is one of the more recent examples of the coach builder's craft, having been constructed for King Edward VII in the second year of the century. It is frequently used when overseas Heads of State visit Britain and although it can be closed during inclement weather, it is usually seen open, to enable the public to get the best possible view of its occupants. Its most recent passengers have been the Duke and Duchess of York, who travelled in it from Westminster Abbey after their wedding on 23 July 1986, and it is easily recognisable from the other coaches because it is painted in a slightly lighter shade of maroon. As it is usually seen open, its rich crimson satin upholstery immediately catches the eye. There is an abundance of gold leaf on the coach and it is usually drawn by six grey postilion horses.

When ambassadors, newly appointed to the Court of St James's, go to Buckingham Palace to present their credentials to Her Majesty, they arrive in *Queen Alexandra's State Coach*. This carriage derives its name from the fact that it was originally used by Queen Alexandra when she was Princess of Wales. It was returned to her at Marlborough House for her continued use after the death of her husband, King Edward VII. It is also seen at every State Opening of Parliament, when it is used to carry the Imperial State Crown from Buckingham Palace to the House of Lords, which is then brought into the robing room by the Comptroller of the Lord Chamberlain's Office. An unusual aspect of Queen Alexandra's State Coach is that the attendants are always The Queen's Bargemaster and one Waterman. This tradition dates from the days when the crown was transported via the Thames from the Tower of London to the Palace of Westminster.

Another example of twentieth-century coach building is the beautiful *Glass Coach*, which is used for nearly all royal weddings. Like the Scottish State Coach it has large picture windows and for occasions when it is important for the occupants to be seen clearly its attraction is self-evident. The Glass Coach was the one chosen by the Princess of Wales for the drive to St Paul's Cathedral on her wedding day and the first glimpse the world had of the bride in her wedding dress was in this elegant, airy carriage as she left Clarence House with her father, Earl Spencer. This journey was one that posed a delicate problem for the Crown Equerry. He had arranged the timetable so that everyone would arrive at St Paul's at exactly the right moment, and he had gone over the route, with stop-watch in hand, many times before the day. On the evening before the wedding he heard that the then Lady Diana wished to exercise the bride's prerogative of arriving late at the church. It was a dilemma. In all the years he had been in royal service, he had never allowed the programme to run late and he was justly proud of his record. The problem was if the bride had her way, the world would see that the time-table had been thrown out – and yet how could he refuse the future Princess of Wales what seemed to her a very reasonable request? The solution was a masterly piece of diplomatic compromise. The bride did arrive late at St Paul's, but the delay was so small hardly anyone noticed. She was satisfied and the royal record for punctuality was preserved.

Among the other coaches and carriages in the Royal Mews are the Town Coach, used by the Sergeants-at-Arms in the processions to and from the State Opening of Parliament; the State Landaus, which are used by various members of the Royal Family in State processions and the Semi-State Landaus, of which five are still in use. All five were built during the reign of Queen Victoria, though it's doubtful if she would have been amused to see the way in which one was decorated after the wedding of the Prince and Princess of Wales: as the royal couple left Buckingham Palace on the first leg of their honeymoon journey, their Semi-State Landau was seen to be sporting a number of balloons and 'Just Married' messages, tied on by Prince Andrew and Prince Edward.

The lightest carriages in the Royal Mews are the two barouches. They are roughly the equivalent of the modern sports car and Queen Elizabeth the Queen Mother is seen to arrive in one of these at Horse Guards every year when she attends the sovereign's Birthday Parade.

The Mews stables are home to some thirty horses – the bays which are used every day and the famous Windsor Greys which always pull The Queen's coach on ceremonial occasions. The horse The Queen rides side-saddle for the ceremony of Trooping the Colour, during the sovereign's annual Birthday Parade, is the 23-year-old black Canadian mare Burmese. Throughout the year Burmese is kept at Windsor and used as a police horse; then a couple of months before the Birthday Parade she is brought to the Royal Mews and ridden every day by a niece of the Crown Equerry to get her used to being handled by a lady, and on the morning of the Parade she is ridden for a couple of hours before Her Majesty takes over, to settle her down.

There is a great deal of public interest in The Queen's horses and carriages, and the Royal Mews is open throughout the year on Wednesday and Thursday afternoons from 2 p.m. to 4 p.m., except when the carriages are required for official duties. As well as the cars, horses and State coaches, there is also a fascinating exhibition of the State harness, together with photographs and other items of historic interest. There are also Royal Mews at Windsor, Hampton Court Palace, Sandringham and in Scotland at the Palace of Holyroodhouse in Edinburgh. The famous Ascot Landaus are kept at Windsor, where they are used to carry The Queen and her guests during the procession up the course at the June race meeting and also to return Her Majesty to the Castle from St George's Chapel after the Garter Service. These Landaus are quite distinctive in appearance with basketwork sides and are pulled by four horses.

Adjacent to the Castle at Windsor is a permanent exhibition organised by the Crown Equerry, at which it is possible to see a wide variety of the horse-drawn transport used by the Royal Family.

The first ever royal car was a Daimler bought by Edward VII as Prince of Wales in 1900. It can be seen, together with a number of other royal vehicles, at an exhibition at Sandringham, where there is also a display of some of the items reflecting the Royal Family's love of horse-racing. Whenever The Queen takes part in a State or other royal occasion which involves a procession, the very last vehicle is always a motor car with a single occupant. The Court Circular for that day will list the names of those travelling in each of the carriages and then in the car at the rear it will say: 'The Crown Equerry'. He always travels alone and he is always in the 'back-up' car – just in case anything should go wrong! The only time he is not following the procession in a car is during the sovereign's Birthday Parade, which is the only occasion when Her Majesty appears on horseback in public. Then the Crown Equerry rides slightly behind The Queen and immediately to her left.

THE ROYAL YACHT

Of all the forms of transport used by The Queen and her family, there is no doubt that the most glamorous and romantic is the Royal Yacht *Britannia*. On 79 Commonwealth cruises and 103 State Visits she has steamed over three-quarters of a million miles (1,207,000 km) and made 584 visits to ports at home and abroad.

King Charles II is credited with having introduced yachting to Britain in 1660; the first Royal Yacht, the *Mary*, was a gift to His Majesty from the people of Amsterdam. The term yachting can be misleading. To most people it conjures up pictures of the wealthy using boats purely for pleasure and sport. In this context, *Britannia* is used very little. The only occasions when it is used as a pleasure cruiser is at Cowes once a year, and for the annual summer cruise around the west coast of Britain carrying the Royal Family to their holiday at Balmoral. There have also been three royal honeymoons spent on board: Princess Anne and Captain Mark Phillips, the Prince and Princess of Wales and the Duke and Duchess of York. Only as such does *Britannia* fulfil the term 'Royal Yacht'; at all other times she is used on official duties and wherever she is in use in whatever

112

part of the world, she becomes The Queen's residence.

Britannia was launched in April 1953 by Her Majesty, shortly before her coronation, at John Brown's shipyard on the banks of the River Clyde in Scotland. It cost £2,098,000 to build, which is slightly less than its yearly running costs at the present time. *Britannia* is rather special for a number of reasons. It's the first Royal Yacht to be built with a complete ocean-going capacity – in previous reigns, sovereigns have had to use Royal Navy warships for any extensive overseas tours – and it is the first to be fitted out as an 'official' royal residence so that The Queen can entertain guests on board. *Britannia* also has the distinction of being the last ship in the Royal Navy in which the sailors slept in hammocks, which they did until a refit in 1970, and it's the only ship in the navy whose Captain is an Admiral. Finally, what makes it so special is the fact that *Britannia* is the one royal structure to have been built during the present reign. Most of Britain's monarchs have left their mark by creating a castle or cathedral – *Britannia* is Elizabeth II's contribution to contemporary history, as far as building is concerned.

For the technically minded, the Royal Yacht's gross tonnage is 5769 (5863 t) and it is 412 feet 3 inches (126 m) long and 55 feet (16 m) wide, making it the largest private yacht in the world. It's powered by 12,000-horsepower (8948-kW) turbines, which were converted to diesel fuel in 1984 and continuous cruising speed is 21 knots (39 kph). The hull is dark blue divided by a gold line which was painted in one long continuous shift manned by a team of craftsmen at the Royal Dockyard in Portsmouth, using real gold leaf. Another noticeable characteristic of *Britannia* is that there are no visible external rivets. The ship is held together by the old method, used in the last Royal Yacht, *Victoria and Albert*, of internal butt straps. *Britannia* is fitted with the latest satellite communications equipment so that The Queen is able to be in constant touch with Buckingham Palace wherever she is in the world.

The State or Royal Apartments on board are located aft of the main-deck, with a drawing room, ante-room (where The Queen receives her guests), sitting room and dining room. Immediately above are the royal bedrooms, while below are cabins for Members of the Royal Household. The decoration in the State Apartments, which was chosen personally by The Queen, is in pastel shades and the furniture is a mixture of old and new, with many of the pieces having been brought from *Britannia*'s predecessor the *Victoria and Albert*. There is a small gimballed table which was designed by Prince Albert on which a drink can be placed and no matter how much the ship rolls, the glass always remains level. Of course *Britannia* is fitted with stabilisers so passengers do not have cause to rely on the gimballed table too much these days. However, during the

State Visit to the West Coast of the United States in 1984, the weather was so bad that not even this clever little piece of furniture was able to withstand the gale force winds and a reception planned to take place on board was cancelled and the venue moved to an hotel.

The State Rooms were designed by Sir Hugh Casson, who, after consulting with Her Majesty, chose a light, airy theme throughout. The carpet is silver grey with a profusion of Persian rugs, and among the more historic items on display is a small triangle of white canvas in a glass case. It is part of the White Ensign which was flown by Captain Scott on his ill-fated expedition to the South Pole in 1911 and which was rescued many years later.

The Queen holds a large number of receptions on board *Britannia* to which some 250 guests can be invited. For a formal dinner party the guest list is reduced to fifty-four. An invitation to a function on board the Royal Yacht is highly sought after and The Queen is fully aware that such an event is appreciated far more than an invitation to dinner or drinks at the British Embassy of the country she is visiting. At a dinner party, the guests sit at a large mahogany table, whose principal decoration is a priceless solid gold camel under two palm trees, which was given to The Queen on the occasion of her State Visit to the Gulf States in 1979 by the Sheik of Dubai. The glassware and dinner services are brought especially from Buckingham Palace for the occasion and the menu (a souvenir copy of which is given to guests on their departure) is the responsibility of the Master of the Household and not the Senior Steward in *Britannia*'s crew. One of the highlights of any evening's entertainment when *Britannia* is moored alongside, is the ceremony of 'Beating Retreat' performed by the Royal Marines Band, who are always on duty when The Queen is embarked.

The Admiral who is Captain of the Royal Yacht is called Flag Officer, Royal Yachts (even though today there is only one royal yacht) and he is also a member of The Queen's Household. There are twenty-one officers and 256 ratings carried as regular crew and these are supplemented by staff from Buckingham Palace when members of the Royal Family are on board. The crew are all volunteers and while officers serve for a maximum of three years, some of the yachtsmen have remained with *Britannia* for many years. The longest serving is a Chief Petty Officer who joined six months before *Britannia*'s commissioning in 1952 and was still serving at the end of 1986. As long as the postings fit in with the requirements of the navy, there is no objection to the yachtsmen staying with *Britannia*. Members of the crew do not receive any special privileges or pay for serving the Royal Family but they are allowed to wear the words 'Royal Yacht' on their cap bands and arm flashes. Their badges are white instead of the regulation red and as a mark of respect in memory of Prince Albert, they wear black bows on the back of their tunics. The only officer on board who has anything to distinguish him from any other naval officer is the Lieutenant-Commander, who is Keeper of the Royal Apartments. His uniform buttons are inscribed with the royal cypher. Officers also have one unique privilege which is denied everyone else in the Royal Navy – they always drink the loyal toast standing up, as an additional mark of respect.

Her Majesty is said to be well aware of the disruptive effect on family life that many months at sea can mean, so whenever *Britannia* is in her home port of Portsmouth, the officers and yachtsmen are allowed to invite their families on board for the day, when they are given a tour of the yacht and a party afterwards. The Queen also makes sure that representatives of the crew and their wives are invited to the staff Christmas parties at Windsor Castle, in addition to the Royal Garden Parties at Buckingham Palace.

In the original specification it was stated that *Britannia* could be used as a hospital ship in time of war. There was some criticism that this was not done during the Falklands Campaign in 1982. But the reason was that *Britannia* at that time used different fuel from the rest of the ships in the fleet and to use her would have meant providing a special tanker just to supply her. However, all criticism was stilled in February 1986 when *Britannia* was involved in one of the most dramatic rescues of recent years. The yacht was sailing to New Zealand in readiness for The Queen's visit, when they received a signal that civil war had broken out in the former British Protectorate of Aden in South Yemen and a large number of British refugees were waiting on the beach to be taken to safety. The signal actually arrived in the middle of the annual darts match between the Wardroom and the Petty Officers Mess. *Britannia* immediately got under way for the war zone, having been instructed by The Queen to give whatever assistance they could.

When *Britannia* sailed into the harbour at Aden it was night and the Captain gave orders that the yacht should be floodlit, with 'all flags flying', so there could be no doubt in anyone's mind as to her identity. Hundreds of refugees were huddled on the beach waiting to be rescued and as *Britannia*'s boats were lowered into the water to take the men, women and children out to the Royal Yacht waiting in deeper water, they came under sporadic gunfire from the rebels on shore.

On that first night, 250 people were brought in; many of them possessing only the clothes they stood up in, they had lost everything else. The Admiral's Secretary, Commander Simon Stone, recalled the feeling of astonishment the refugees showed when they realised it was the Royal

Yacht which had come to their aid: 'They simply couldn't believe it at first. Of all the ships in the world to turn up over the horizon, *Britannia* was the last one they had expected.' Once they were safely on board they were moved into every available cabin, including the Royal Apartments – The Queen had issued express instructions that this should be so. Even her own rooms were placed at their disposal. Altogether some 1100 people were rescued and they were then taken to Djibouti where *Britannia* entered the harbour 'dressed overall and with the Royal Marine Band playing "Rule Britannia".' On board were the citizens of many countries. *Brittania*'s original orders had been to rescue British subjects, but as Commander Stone said, 'Once we got there it was impossible to tell who was who, and even if we could have, it would have made no difference. We brought out anyone who wanted to come.'

Once the rescue was over, *Britannia* resumed her voyage to New Zealand with the crew using the time to repair the ravages caused by the unexpected influx of so many guests. For the officers and yachtsmen the incident had come at exactly the right time. For years they had been waiting to prove that *Britannia* was not just another pleasure cruiser, fit only to be used as a floating hotel. At last they could be justly proud of the part she had played in a dangerous and worthwhile operation.

SPORTING INTERESTS

'The aim and objective of everybody who has anything to do with The Queen's racing or breeding is to breed a Derby winner' says Lord Caernarvon, Her Majesty's Racing Manager for the past twenty years. He was speaking at the Highclere Stud in Wiltshire, the nerve centre of all The Queen's racing activities, which keeps her in touch with everything that is happening in the world of horse-racing. There is a computer with a direct link to Kentucky in the United States, the world centre of blood-stock breeding, and if Her Majesty needs information about any horse anywhere in the world, she can have it in a matter of seconds. The computer was a gift from America but The Queen pays for the lines and all the software that is required to keep her in the forefront of one of the most competitive sports in the world.

If racing is the sport of kings, in the case of our present sovereign it is also very much the sport of queens; both Her Majesty and Queen Elizabeth the Queen Mother are passionately fond of racing, but while Queen Elizabeth sticks to the winter aspect of the sport with her hurdlers and steeplechasers, The Queen prefers the pure speed and stamina required for the Flat. Lord Caernarvon believes it is not only because of a preference for the Flat that The Queen has never gone in for competing 'over the sticks': 'I think it's because she realises that Queen Elizabeth enjoys jumping so much and it's marvellous for steeplechasing and hurdling that the Queen Mother is such an enthusiastic patron. She doesn't want to compete with her mother and likewise her mother feels the same way about the Flat as far as The Queen is concerned.'

Her Majesty grew up with horses. She could ride almost as soon as she could walk and some of her earliest memories must be of riding at Sandringham with her father. Her passion for horse-racing developed while she was still Princess Elizabeth and one of the wedding gifts she received in 1947 was a filly named Astrakhan from the Aga Khan. The filly also became the first of her many winners when it won at Hurst Park in 1949. But it was when Princess Elizabeth become Queen that her interest in racing was able to be fully realised. The Royal Studs became her property on the death of her father, King George VI, and Her Majesty immediately set about becoming the outstanding owner and breeder she is today.

117

The Queen is not just another successful owner who pays for the horses and then sits back and lets somebody else make the decisions. She is keenly interested in every aspect of her string and she is regarded as being one of the world's experts. Her Racing Manager has no doubts at all about his employer's qualifications:

She is as professionally knowledgeable as anyone in racing. She is an extremely good judge of pedigrees; she is a very good judge of an individual horse in terms of make and shape; and she is an extremely good judge–when she is able to be there–of reading a race and an awful lot of people are bad judges at reading a race. So she's got all three put together really.

The set-up in The Queen's Racing Stables is that Lord Caernarvon is the Racing Manager, with overall responsibility for everything to do with Her Majesty's racing programme – the buying, selling and the breeding. Then there are two trainers, Ian Balding and Dick Hearne, and they have total responsibility for the horses. They discuss with Lord Caernarvon the entries for the various races and once they have reached agreement, the recommendations are put to The Queen, who always makes the final decision. It means a great deal of time is spent on the telephone. Lord Caernarvon speaks to Her Majesty at least three or four times a week during the season, when they talk about the chances of one of her horses running the following day or assessing the opposition, and then – equally important – keeping Her Majesty informed about the results. Lord Caernarvon says that wherever she is, The Queen is thinking about her thoroughbreds and awaiting a call to find out how they have run. It could be at Holyroodhouse, Windsor or even on board *Britannia*. The chain of command is fairly informal and if The Queen wants to know something about the condition or performance of one of her horses she is just as likely to pick up the telephone and talk to Ian Balding or Dick Hearne directly. There is an easy camaraderie among the racing fraternity and even though no one is ever in danger of forgetting that The Queen is who she is, they speak to each other as professional equals, with no one afraid to voice an opinion just because it might be unpopular. Inevitably there is the occasional disagreement between owner and Racing Manager because, as Lord Caernarvon says, 'I wouldn't be doing my job properly if I didn't base my decisions on what I consider to be my best judgement of a situation. The Queen will sometimes query something I may have suggested or vice versa, but most of the time we agree.'

The 'bible' of the racing world is *The Sporting Life*, the daily newspaper which gives details of all the previous day's results and the prospects for the current day's calendar. It is required reading at The Queen's breakfast table and Her Majesty also has a comprehensive collection of form books, which she is able to consult whenever she needs to know something about runners and riders, results and performances. If there is one difference between The Queen and other major owners, Lord Caernarvon thinks it is in her attitude to selling: 'It is sometimes harder to make her sell something she rather likes than it would be for somebody else involved commercially in racing, but usually she takes the advice.'

The Queen is an active buyer of horses but in the past few years she has not bought many yearlings, mainly because of the prices being paid by the Arab syndicates and the multi-million-pound deals of owners such as Mr Robert Sangster. When Her Majesty has bought a female in order to change the line it has usually been for a bargain price. It is important to understand that the whole of The Queen's racing activities is privately financed – by the sale of animals out of training; by the sale of brood mares; or by the sale of nominations to The Queen's stallions. Lord Caernarvon is emphatic about the fact that not a single penny comes out of public funds: 'We have absolutely no involvement with the Civil List at all. We are entirely and completely private. The stables are run on commercial terms and we have to make a budget to see what the year ahead is going to cost and try to keep above the red line.' The fact that The Queen is one of the most successful owners and breeders of racehorses in the world is a tribute to her own and her advisers' knowledge and good business sense. Lord Caernarvon says, 'In terms of the financing of the racing and breeding operation, we are very much in profit and what's more I think we have every chance of breeding a Derby winner for The Queen.'

If horses figure largely in the overall sporting picture of the Royal Family it is understandable. The tradition of equestrian excellence in Britain's royalty is as established as the monarchy itself. The Queen was given her first pony at the age of three by her uncle the late Duke of Windsor. Both Prince Charles and Princess Anne started their riding lessons before their fourth birthdays and the latest generation of royal horsemen, Peter Phillips and Prince William of Wales, were both in the saddle by the time they were three years old. The Duke and Duchess of York rode their ponies together at Windsor in their pre-teens and even the Princess of Wales, who has a well-known aversion to horses following a fall as a child, has been seen riding with The Queen in the grounds at Sandringham.

The most successful sporting competitor in the Royal Family is Princess Anne. She was the first member to win an international title when she became European Three-Day-Event Champion at Burghley in September 1971, riding The Queen's horse Doublet; and she was the first member of the Royal Family to be chosen to take part in an Olympic Games when she competed for Britain at Montreal in 1976. The Princess had been competing at local events since she was a child and one of the difficulties when she entered top-class competitions such as Badminton was that some people refused to take her seriously at first, thinking that because she was The Queen's daughter she would expect preferential treatment. History has recorded that she did not expect any special treatment – and she certainly did not get any. Within a remarkably short time she had reached the pinnacle of her sport, becoming European Champion, which meant virtually World Champion at the time, when she was still only twenty-one. Even she felt that perhaps this was a little bit rapid: 'In some ways it came a bit soon in my eventing career. It was really only three years after I'd started seriously and people did tend to say things like "Oh, you've had it now. Girls are only ever successful on one horse, so you might as well stop now while the going is good", which seemed a bit premature I thought.' Quite an understatement when you remember that Her Royal Highness went on to win a silver medal in another European Championship (on a different horse, Goodwill) before being chosen – on merit alone – for the British team at the Olympic Games. It was in Montreal that she demonstrated her determination and courage when she remounted and finished one of the toughest cross-country courses after falling at fence number thirty-six, where she suffered severe concussion and massive bruising. Since 1976 her increasing load of public duties and the birth of two children have prevented her from reaching such heights again but she has remained an active competitor in events up and down the country and if the right horse could be found she might easily be selected at international level once more.

In recent years Princess Anne has joined the ranks of lady jockeys. On St George's Day 1985 she climbed into the saddle for her first race on the flat over the one-and-a-half-mile (2·4-km) Derby course at Epsom. The occasion was a charity race in aid of Riding for the Disabled, of which the Princess has been Patron since 1970, and her mount was Against the Grain. Her Royal Highness had been working hard with trainer David Nicholson for some weeks before the race and on the day she came a creditable fourth. When she was asked after the race if she wanted to race again she replied, 'You are not likely to see me in the royal colours.' However, she has appeared a number of times since and with the determination to succeed that has been the hallmark of her riding career, she ended up in the winner's enclosure just over a year later when she rode Gulfland to a five-lengths victory at Redcar in Yorkshire. The race was the Mommessin Amateur Riders' Stakes and the Princess was riding a 5–1 outsider. She beat the odds-on favourite Positive and was presented with a magnum of champagne for her victory – not too useful to someone who never drinks any alcohol at all! It was the Princess's thirteenth race and afterwards when she was asked if she planned to continue riding she said: 'As long as the owners are prepared to allow idiots like me to ride.'

Princess Anne met her husband Captain Mark Phillips through their mutual love of horses. He was already an Olympic rider when they were introduced in 1968 and he has gone on to become one of the world's outstanding equestrian performers, winning Badminton four times. Mark is sponsored by the Range Rover Team and his competitive year is divided between the major events in Britain, America and Australia. He also teaches young riders under a scholarship scheme and he is in constant demand at riding seminars in various parts of the world. With parents of such ability, it was inevitable that both Zara and Peter Phillips would grow up in the saddle, and they were both riding ponies almost as soon as they could walk. Peter has already started competing in Pony Club events and if he or his sister show the slightest spark of talent they won't have far to look for encouragement and sound advice.

At the age of eighty-six, Queen Elizabeth the Queen Mother is not only one of the world's favourite grandmothers but also probably Britain's favourite owner of racehorses. No one has done more to popularise the sport of National Hunt racing than Her Majesty and her racing colours of pale blue and buff have been first past the winning post more than 300 times. Her popularity is such that it has been estimated that an entry by one of her horses can mean an extra 1000 on the gate at a winter meeting. Her Majesty takes an extraordinary interest in all her ten horses in training and if her public duties allow she will turn out in the most atrocious weather to see them run. As with other members of the Royal Family, Queen Elizabeth does not seem to mind extremes of cold or heat and in the sub-zero temperatures of January and February, she can still frequently be seen at Sandown Park, Windsor or Ascot if one of her horses is running.

Her Majesty's interest in the sport began back in 1949 when she bought her first racehorse, Monaveen. The purchase price was £1000 and the horse was shared with her daughter, then Princess Elizabeth. During those early years Dick Francis, now one of the world's best-selling authors, was the leading jockey for Peter Cazalet, at that time Queen Elizabeth's trainer. He rode many winners for his royal patron but he will always be remembered for one race he lost. On 24 March 1956, Francis was riding the Queen Mother's famous 'chaser Devon Loch in the Grand National. The horse was a mere fifty yards or so from the winning post, way out in front with nothing between it and the richest prize in National Hunt racing, when without any warning its legs splayed out, the horse collapsed and Francis was thrown to the ground. The former royal jockey said later he was told by those who had been with the Queen Mother that

121

'She never turned a hair.' There was no sign of what she must have been feeling inside over the failure and collapse of a valuable and dearly loved horse, or of the disappointment and frustration after losing one of the greatest races in the world. Her concern was entirely for the horse and for those who had looked after him – the trainer, jockey and stable lad. It was the most perfect display of royal dignity and manners.

When Peter Cazalet died in 1973, Fulke Walwyn was approached to become the Queen Mother's principal trainer. He said, 'It didn't take me long to make up my mind, it's not the sort of offer you get every day.' As with The Queen and her racing advisers, Queen Elizabeth is in constant touch with Mr Walwyn, talking to him three of four times a week during the season. She is never too busy to hear about one of her horses and Clarence House is the only royal residence in the country which has been equipped with a 'blower' – the special racecourse commentary service which gives the latest information from the courses on betting odds, form, jockeys and most important of all, results. So if Her Majesty is unable to attend a race in person, she is still able to keep fully abreast of what is happening.

For many years the Duke of Edinburgh's favourite sport was polo, to which he was introduced by his uncle the late Earl Mountbatten, but he was forced to give it up by the onset of arthritis so he turned his attention to carriage driving. It is a sport which requires a great deal of mental effort as well as physical strength and the Duke has spent many hours studying the technical and scientific aspects. As with everything else he has undertaken, His Royal Highness decided right from the start that if it was to be done, it had to be done well. That he has succeeded in his aim has been ably demonstrated by the fact that shortly before he approached his sixtieth birthday, he led a Great Britain team to the World Championships and even today he is regarded as one of the top ten drivers in the world.

More than a hundred years ago, the sport of polo was introduced to England and since then it has become an established favourite with generations of royalty. King George V as Prince George was the first member of the British Royal Family to play polo, when he played in Argentina in 1881, where it had already become the national game. Lord Mountbatten and the late Duke of Windsor, as Prince of Wales, took up the sport enthusiastically and when they both toured India in the 1920s their enthusiasm developed into a passion. Lord Mountbatten said polo was like a naval battle, drawing on the same qualities of 'leadership, decisiveness, speed and communications, manoeuvrability and good fast shooting'. Mountbatten passed his love of the game on to his nephew Philip, who was also encouraged by King George VI, another keen player.

The Duke of Edinburgh is credited with doing for polo what his daughter Princess Anne has done for Three-Day Eventing: turning it from an élitist sport for the very rich into a popular spectator sport. He was elected President of the Household Brigade Polo Club at Windsor Great Park, now the Guards Polo Club, and immediately opened Smith's Lawn to the public on Sunday afternoons. This was, and continues to be, a great success, partly because of the attraction of the game, but more so because of the possibility of seeing members of the Royal Family at close quarters.

The Duke introduced his eldest son Charles to the game when the latter was just fourteen and it has remained the heir to the throne's favourite sport ever since. He plays regularly for The Windsor Park Team whose shirts are green with red trim; for Les Diables Bleus in their all-blue strip; and for The Maple Leafs, whose shirts are red with a white maple leaf. The Prince of Wales has also turned out for the Royal Navy at Tidworth.

Polo may now be a popular spectator sport but it is still an expensive game to play. Each pony costs around £3000 a year to keep and the Prince has thirteen, of which his favourite is a chestnut mare called Happiness. They are kept in the Royal Mews at Windsor, where they are looked after by Prince Charles's groom, Raoul Correa, who was born in Argentina but who has been a British citizen for more than twelve years. Princess Diana dutifully follows her husband when he is playing polo but she has let it be known that horses are not her favourite animals. The new Duchess of York, however, is an experienced horsewoman, having virtually grown up in the saddle. Her father Major Ronnie Ferguson is the Royal Family's Polo Manager and as a former officer in The Life Guards was an accomplished polo player himself in his younger days.

Horses apart, the Duke of Edinburgh is also a dedicated sailor who competed at Cowes for many years with his old friend and sailing tutor, the late Uffa Fox. He still makes sure that *Britannia* is always available during the first week of August as the flagship of the Royal Yacht Squadron for Cowes Week and he is usually among the first of the Royal Family to sail as crew in one of the racing craft.

One sport in which the Prince and Princess of Wales do share an interest is swimming. They both try to swim every day and Princess Diana in particular is known for her love of the water. The Prince has tried his hand at many other pursuits including wind-surfing and angling, while in the winter months he hunts regularly with the Beaufort Hunt in the Gloucestershire countryside near his home, Highgrove House. Another of the Prince and Princess of Wales' mutual sporting pleasure is skiing. They both especially enjoy the challenge of the slopes at Maldun in Liechtenstein, which are testing enough to skiers of their experience, but one of the biggest problems is the constant presence of the world's Press all trying to get a picture of them falling over.

The Queen's youngest son Prince Edward is a true all-rounder. He plays a wide variety of sports and says that as far as he is concerned the main thing is to be able to take part: 'I enjoy a lot of sports and I prefer playing to watching. Sport is something to do rather than watch in my case.' His favourite game is rugby football which he started playing at school when he was eleven. In his early days as a player he occupied one of the toughest positions on the field – hooker, right in the middle of the scrum – but as he said later, 'I very quickly grew out of that position and became a "prop", and since then I've played in every position in the forwards. Occasionally I go back to being a hooker for seven-a-side tournaments and I enjoy it a great deal.' With his height and weight – he is well over six feet (1·8 m) – he is ideally suited to the game, but when at Cambridge he became the target for a lot of unwelcome attention from some of the opposing teams. As he put it: 'Apparently there was a "Get Edward Society" the object of which was to see who could inflict the most injuries on me in any one match.' At first he took it in good part as one of the penalties of being a member of the Royal Family, but within a comparatively short time it became increasingly obvious that some of the tackles he was being subjected to were carried with a serious intention of doing him injury, so reluctantly he had to give up playing rugby in his last year at university. Being an active man he needed an outlet for his energy, so he took up the ancient game of 'real' or 'royal' tennis which he plays at Hampton Court Palace, on the court built by Henry VIII.

The Prince also shares his father's enthusiasm for carriage driving and is frequently seen lending a hand with the harness at competitions in which the Duke of Edinburgh is taking part. The Duke taught all his children the rudiments of dinghy sailing when they were still very young and they have all been brought up with a love of and a knowledge of boats. Edward is a keen sailor and learnt this skill on the waters of Loch Muick in Scotland near Balmoral. Princess Anne once said that if the time ever came when she could no longer compete in Three-Day Events, she would probably take to sailing seriously; she has crewed for her father many times and if her attitude to sailing is anything like her attitude to riding, she could well be competing at international level in this sport too if she does take it up seriously.

Prince Andrew, now Duke of York, is another of The Queen's sons to whom rugby was a first love. He played at school and also when he first entered the navy at the Royal Naval College, Dartmouth. He was considered to be a tough, robust player who could 'give it as well as take it' and he said that one of the attractions of the game was that 'you could get up to all sorts of things in the scrum'. In fact His Royal Highness's first public engagement was to speak at a rugby dinner in London when he shared the platform with such rugby luminaries as Dr Tony O'Reilly of

Ireland and Cliff Morgan, the legendary Welsh outside-half. Prince Andrew likes the company of rugby players; he is comfortable in their presence and enjoys the rough, sometimes crude humour of after-match parties.

Prince Andrew is also an expert shot, having been introduced to guns at a very early age by the Duke of Edinburgh during the annual New Year pheasant shoots at Sandringham. All the members of the Royal Family, male and female, can handle a gun, but The Queen contents herself these days with following the guns rather than taking part herself, despite the fact that her father made sure both she and Princess Margaret were proficient as soon as they were big enough to learn the skills safely. The Duke of York, however, is an enthusiast and rarely misses an opportunity of a day's shooting. Every year he takes part in a charity match organised by former racing-driver Jackie Stewart, in which two teams compete against each other with the proceeds from the event going to the Save the Children Fund. Stewart is an old friend of Princess Anne and Captain Mark Phillips (his wife Helen is Zara Phillips's godmother) and the team usually consists of: Mark Phillips; the Duke of York; the Duke of Kent and King Constantine. The opposing team is made up of celebrities from sport, the acting profession and other members of the Royal Family, including the Hon. Angus Ogilvy (husband of Princess Alexandra) with their wives usually acting as loaders. The event attracts a large crowd who have a unique opportunity of mixing informally with royalty and the other celebrities.

As far as The Queen's sporting interests are concerned, inevitably her horses have taken precedence over anything else, and although she enjoys a variety of pastimes, affairs of State have made it impossible for her to be more than an interested spectator on most occasions. It is a little known fact that when The Queen was a young girl she hunted regularly with the Pytchley. Of course in those days there was rarely any adverse publicity about 'blood sports' and it was considered a normal part of a well-to-do young lady's upbringing. However, the then Pricess Elizabeth did not show any great enthusiasm for the sport and she did not continue to take part in her adult life. Her Majesty has maintained her enthusiasm for riding and one of her greatest pleasures is to ride for a couple of hours at Windsor or Sandringham. Similarly, she is a great patron of Three-Day Eventing and the Royal Family's presence is always guaranteed at Badminton, which she has supported since its beginning.

The Queen is also a successful pigeon fancier. This is a sport she inherited along with the Royal Pigeon Loft at Sandringham on her accession to the throne. It is a sport more usually associated with working-class areas in the North of England, but Her Majesty has supported it with her traditional enthusiasm and she has been very successful in races both at home and overseas.

Dogs play an important part in the lifestyle of all the Royal Family and even though Corgis are the breed usually associated with The Queen by the public, her own preference is for gun dogs. She breeds Black Labradors at Sandringham, from where they are sold throughout the world. Her Majesty is highly skilled in gun dog events and even though her position precludes her from participating in public shows (the security aspect alone makes the possibility a policeman's nightmare), she sometimes takes an active part in private gun dog trials at Sandringham, where neighbouring farmers and workers on the royal estates can guarantee the discretion the sovereign needs on such occasions. Her Majesty has demonstrated an expertise which has placed her in the ranks of the professional handlers and judges. In 1984 she acted as a judge at the Kennel Club's two-day Retriever Trial, which was held at Sandringham. The Queen had invited the Kennel Club to hold the event on her land and when they in turn invited her to act as one of the judges she accepted with one proviso: there was to be no advance publicity. So the first the competitors knew of their royal host's participation was when her name appeared on the meeting card of the day. The invitation had not been offered as a gesture to The Queen because the trials were being held at Sandringham; the gun dog authorities take their responsibilities too seriously for that. They were well aware of Her Majesty's knowledge and skill as a handler and it was her reputation as an expert on gun dogs which prompted the move. Unlike the other members of her family, The Queen does not favour water sports. She is known not to be a good sailor and apart from official voyages aboard the Royal Yacht, the only time she voluntarily uses *Britannia* is for the annual summer cruise around the west coast of Britain en route to Scotland for her holiday at Balmoral. Her Majesty was taught to swim as a girl but she does not use the pool at Buckingham Palace as frequently as some of the other members. She does still enjoy stalking when in Scotland, but unlike her mother and eldest son, she does not care for fishing at all. She has said that the idea of standing in a cold river up to her waist in water for hours on end holds little appeal and it is not that the cold or damp worries her: one of her greatest pleasures is to walk alone in the hills above Balmoral, accompanied only by one or two of the dogs who are never far from her side.

THE PUBLIC IMAGE

Some sections of the British Press have had so much royal coverage that, not unnaturally, they're looking for different slants and tend to concentrate on what I would consider trivia. The fact that individual members of the Royal Family go up and down in so-called popular esteem is in my mind very much an invention of the newspapers themselves – the members of the Royal Family do not change their characters.

So says Michael Shea, Press Secretary to The Queen and the man with one of the most difficult jobs in the Royal Household and, some would say, the most thankless. The Press Secretary is one of The Queen's closest aides. He is in daily contact with her and other members of the Royal Family, and he has direct access to Her Majesty. If he needs to speak to her either on the telephone or in person, he does not have to obtain the permission of the Private Secretary or go through any other third party. It is a unique and privileged position, but one which carries with it the responsibility for all news emanating from Buckingham Palace – and there's a great deal of that!

Michael Shea is in fact only the eighth person to hold the office of Press Secretary since Mr F. J. Prior was appointed in 1918. In 1931, King George V decided he had no use for a Press Secretary and the post was abolished, with what few Press matters there were being attended to by the Assistant Private Secretary of the day. But in 1944, King George VI realised the importance of good public relations and re-established the position. From that day on there has always been a Press Secretary and now Mr Shea has two Assistant Press Secretaries to help him deal with the queries which arrive at the Palace twenty-four hours a day, 365 days a year, from all over the world.

Michael Shea looks after the affairs of The Queen himself, accompanying her on all State visits abroad and overseeing the media requirements for every major State occasion, as well as annual events such as The Queen's Christmas Day broadcast. The two Assistant Press Secretaries report directly to him but in practice they have their own responsibilities which are divided in the following way. The number two in the office, John Haslam, looks after the Press affairs of Princess Anne, Prince Andrew and Prince Edward; Victor Chapman, the other Assistant Press Secretary, works practically full time for the Prince and Princess of Wales. Nevertheless, both he and John Haslam are employed by The Queen as

her Assistant Press Secretaries, and it is to Her Majesty that their ultimate responsibility lies.

The Queen Mother and Princess Margaret have their own Press Secretary, Major John Griffin, who works from Clarence House, while
Princess Alexandra, the Duke of Kent and the Duke of Gloucester each
has a Private Secretary who handles Press enquiries on their behalf. The
Press Office at Buckingham Palace is insistent on one issue: it does not
involve itself in any way with the affairs of Prince and Princess Michael
of Kent. This is because Prince Michael, The Queen's cousin, gave up
his place in the line of succession to the throne on his marriage to a
Roman Catholic.

Visitors to the Press Office at Buckingham Palace are surprised to find
that its entire complement is only seven people. It consists of the three
Press Secretaries and four lady clerks, one or two of whom have been
there for more than twenty years and who would be more than competent
to act as Press Secretary should the need arise. But women in the Royal
Household have not been very successful in climbing to the top. In fact,
only one has ever risen to the rank of Assistant Press Secretary and she
was Mrs Michael Wall, who worked in the Press Office for twenty-seven
years before her retirement. She was passed over for promotion several
times during her stay at the Palace, each time for a man. She knew she
would never become Press Secretary to the sovereign and accepted the
fact. It seems to be a man's world around The Queen.

Although the office of Press Secretary is a comparatively new one in the
Royal Household, there has been an official called the Court Newsman
since the days of King George III. His Majesty became so annoyed with
what he called the inaccurate reporting of the movements of the Royal
Family that he appointed someone whose sole duty was to distribute the
Court Circular, which newspapers were required to publish with not a
single word changed or omitted. The earliest records in the Buckingham
Palace files show that in 1899, the Court Newsman's duties included
attending personally at Buckingham Palace every day, both afternoon
and evening when Queen Victoria was in London, and once a day
(Sundays included) when Her Majesty was away from London. He was
also required to attend any Court functions at St James's Palace and
Buckingham Palace, and during the Court season he reported to the Lord
Chamberlain's Office a number of days before State balls or concerts,
where he would sit down and personally copy out the invitation lists.
Similarly, after 'levees and drawing rooms', he was given the invitation
cards so that he could make lists to deliver at the offices of the various
newspapers. In 1886, his salary for these duties amounted to £45 a year,
but even this sum was considered excessive and in 1909 it was reduced to

£20. However, the position was not as badly rewarded as it appears because the newspapers, even then, were prepared to pay the Court Newsman for information about royalty and an enterprising official could make a steady living out of the tit-bits he sent to his favourite editors. Strangely enough, this practice was not frowned upon by the sovereign and it was recognised by the Royal Household as a legitimate way for the Court Newsman to enlarge his meagre earnings. Also, a number of ambitious ladies and gentlemen who wanted their names to appear in the same column as The Queen would quietly slip him the odd guinea so that he wouldn't forget them. The position of Court Newsman cannot have been as humble as one might suppose, for there was certainly a lot of competition for the job, and nepotism was an accepted route to appointment. The first Court Newsman was a Mr Doane and the next name the records show as occupying the post was a Mr Beard who was a grandson of Mr Doane. Mr Beard served until 1886 and was succeeded by Mr A. Phillips who, in 1889, handed over to his son Mr W. Phillips, who was to look after Court Press matters until 1909 (when the salary was reduced to £20 per year). The last Court Newsman was Mr H. C. North and he served until 1918 when the office of Press Secretary was established. The Court Newsman worked under the jurisdiction of the Master of the Household and, to this day, the Court Circular containing the engagements of the Royal Family for the previous day, which *The Times* and the *Daily Telegraph* publish every morning, comes not from the Press Office but still from the office of the Master of the Household. It is a chore that the Press Secretary is delighted not to have to do, especially when there is a long list of foreign visitors to Buckingham Palace, each of whose names has to be checked and rechecked for the correct spelling.

Of course, the business of reporting royal events has changed almost beyond recognition since those days of King George III, even in the past twenty years. The comings and goings, the romances, marriages and divorces of the Royal Family have become the required daily reading for millions of people, not only in Britain, but throughout the world. Writing on the Royal Family has become big business and many of the journalists and authors who have joined the 'royal watchers' squad have become rich and famous personalities in their own right.

Sir Alastair Burnet of Independent Television News was the envy of the world of royal journalism when he was chosen to interview the Prince and Princess of Wales at their home in Kensington Palace. The film of the interview was sold to a large number of countries and was shown in America at peak time, coast to coast, achieving audience figures even greater than the current leading soap operas *Dallas* and *Dynasty*. Burnet wrote a book based on the interview, which was published in record time to coincide with the television programme. The sales are said to have made him a rich man – and one of the Prince of Wales' charities benefited to the tune of several hundred thousand pounds. The Palace was so pleased with the results that Burnet was again selected to present an intimate television portrait of the royal couple a year later. By now he had become one of the world's experts on the Royal Family, with a newly established reputation, eclipsing anything he had previously achieved in a long and distinguished career in journalism.

Another royal reporter, one with not nearly the same amount of approval from Buckingham Palace, is James Whitaker of the *Daily Mirror*. He is one of the highest-paid journalists in Fleet Street and for some years he has been concentrating on royal events, because, as he says, 'One day my editor sent me to cover a royal engagement and I found myself drinking champagne and eating smoked salmon. From that day on I decided this was the life for me.' Whitaker has been around the royal scene for such a long time that members of the Family have come to know him quite well. As he puts it:

I don't actually get my feet under any of their tables and sit down and have a meal with them, but I have been to a number of receptions and cocktail parties where they have been present, and even if they don't always approve of what I write, I am quite sure there isn't a single member of the Royal Family who doesn't know me well – and certainly they all recognise me.

This is all very different from the way in which the BBC's Godfrey Talbot worked when he started to cover royal events. Talbot was the first correspondent appointed by the BBC to be 'an observer of royal events' shortly after the Second World War, when reporters were regarded as little more than tradesmen at Buckingham Palace. He recalls his early days as a royal reporter:

It was a quite different world then. Different climate of opinion, different climate of morals and of behaviour. As far as the Royal Family was concerned, journalism consisted of controlled and modest chronicling of the official engagements and ceremonial. It was a world removed from today's frenzied Press presences. The Press Secretary was one of the last of the old courtiers, the legendary Commander Richard Colville. He was ex-Royal Navy, punctilious, prickly but with beautiful manners – and almost no knowledge whatever of newspapers and journalism. He was well meaning but he didn't know what news was all about – and didn't want to know! Any enquiry about what The Queen felt about a particular subject, or even what she might be doing, apart from a public engagement, was met with the comment, 'That is a private matter, I'm sorry, I can't help at all.' His main job, as he saw it, was to protect the sovereign from these suspicious characters, these dubious figures, the Pressmen. Indeed, most of Fleet Street gave up telephoning the Press Office at Buckingham Palace and Commander Colville became known as 'the abominable No-Man'.

On the surface, this seems completely different from the way in which the

Press Office operates today. The telephones never seem to stop ringing and each enquiry is greeted with a polite answer, even if the person at the other end cannot give the information you need. Grania Forbes was a 'royal watcher' for more than ten years: first of all as Court Correspondent for the Press Association, which meant she was accredited to Buckingham Palace and was welcomed there every morning; more recently, however, she wrote on royal events for the *Daily Mail*, where the requirements were slightly different.

I think Buckingham Palace's attitude is very much the same. They are in a difficult position in that they have to gauge just how much information they release and how much they keep to themselves. Obviously one of the problems is that the mystery of majesty must be maintained. The Queen is Head of State. She is not in show business, though at times we tend to treat her as if she is.

Michael Shea is quick to point out that members of the Royal Family do not compete in the 'ratings war' and do not consider themselves as players in a real-life soap opera.

There is an extremely arrogant statement which keeps being made by one or two so-called 'royal watchers', who say that if it wasn't for them the Royal Family would be terribly worried and if they didn't do their job, the popularity of the monarchy would fade away overnight. Well I think everybody would agree that's total rubbish. The monarchy to survive does not need the sort of prurient and/or sometimes quite adulatory coverage it gets.

But the very existence of a Press Secretary as one of The Queen's closest advisers indicates that the Royal Family takes more than a passing interest in what is being said and written about them. Ronald Allison was in a unique position to judge the Royal Family's attitude to the Press. He was the BBC's Court Correspondent for five years and then moved into Buckingham Palace as Press Secretary to The Queen in 1973, so he was able to see the situation from both sides. 'The Queen was very aware of what was being said about her in the Press,' he remembers. 'She always took a great interest in what was happening and she would frequently ask why a certain event had been reported in a particular way – or sometimes, why something had not been covered.'

Both the Duke of Edinburgh and Princess Anne have had their differences with the Press in the past. The Princess's 'naff-off' remarks to photographers who had caught her at a bad moment have become part of Fleet Street folklore and when her father found a boat load of Pressmen sailing too close to his dinghy off the Isle of Wight, his language was of the kind not to be reported in family newspapers. These days, however, he seems to have arrived at a fairly peaceful truce with the Press. Most of the Duke of Edinburgh's comments are about wildlife preservation or the environment and his opinions are often shared by the majority, so there is rarely a question of contentious issues being aired publicly.

Princess Anne has recently become the subject of much favourable Press attention because of her work as President of the Save the Children Fund. When she addressed the Sportswriters of Great Britain after they had voted her their Personality of the Year, she took the opportunity of mending a few fences in her acceptance speech: '. . . I wouldn't dream of complaining about you, as you are only doing your jobs – editors, as we all know, would lose them if they didn't get a picture or a story. And if the story is done properly you cannot be popular with everybody all of the time.' Then came the sting in the tail: 'Anyway, you do tend to be rather a touchy lot when it comes to talking about you.' When the Prince and Princess of Wales visited America in 1985, more than a thousand reporters and cameramen applied for accreditation to cover the tour. And the previous year The Queen's visit to the West Coast of America received more coverage than the last Presidential election. Why should this be? What is this fascination world-wide with the British Royal Family? Is it just gossip and the fact that so many of us like to hear tittle-tattle about the most famous family in the world? Are we genuinely interested in the serious aspects of the monarchy, or just the behind-the-scenes activities? Why should this curiosity extend overseas as well as being prevalent in Britain? Many of these questions are simply part of the inexplicable mystery of monarchy. The fact remains that nowadays nothing sells newspapers or magazines like royalty. A survey of national periodicals in Britain in 1985 showed that a photograph of The Queen or the Princess of Wales on the cover could mean an increase in sales by as much as ten per cent. Ten years ago a similar survey showed that pictures of Princess Margaret or Princess Anne could have exactly the opposite effect. There are now several monthly magazines devoted exclusively to royalty. The most successful is *Majesty*, whose editor Ingrid Seward says she gets letters from all over the world commenting on the articles and photographs she publishes in the magazine: 'And if we make a mistake there's an absolute deluge of mail from readers who are experts on every aspect of the Royal Family.'

In Europe publishers tend to look for the sensational headline, rather than the real facts. One German magazine has had The Queen supposedly deposed seven times; an attempt on Prince Philip's life made four times; Princess Anne's marriage to Captain Mark Phillips has reputedly broken up every year since they were married in 1973; and Princess Margaret has apparently been treated for every disease from hepatitis to alcoholism. The French like to know about the romantic side of the Royal Family with 'insider' stories about the love-life of the Prince and Princess of Wales and, until his wedding in July 1986 to Miss Sarah

Ferguson, about Prince Andrew and the latest girl in his life. When Prince Edward was at Cambridge he was dogged by a couple of persistent reporters trying to catch him with a girl-friend. They even tried to bribe several of his fellow students into telling them what went on in the privacy of his rooms. One or two astute would-be entrepreneurs, who had not even met the Prince, enhanced their university grants by inventing lurid tales of royal capers, which were consumed voraciously by the gullible reporters.

In Australia and New Zealand there is an almost fanatical interest in the Royal Family. Lynn Bell is an Australian journalist based in London, from where she reports for the Fairfax group of papers and magazines. She explained the difficulties in being a foreign correspondent in London trying to obtain up-to-the-minute stories about royalty for her readers back in Australia:

The Australians have been traditionally interested in the Royal Family as a family and probably the only time any single person in the Family came in for more coverage than the others was when the Princess of Wales came on the scene. You couldn't open a newspaper or magazine in Australia or New Zealand without seeing her picture on the front page. 'Dianamania' hit us as hard as any country in the world. Now we've got it a little more into perspective and if we run a good solid story on just about any of the royals it has the same impact.

What about getting help from Buckingham Palace? Are they as interested in having coverage abroad as at home? Lynn Bell says it is difficult:

It's a funny situation. There are certain questions which you are longing to ask, but you know if you do ask, you won't get an answer. Then there are the questions you dare not ask because you might upset them and if you are going to keep on doing your job you need a good relationship with the Palace. So the answer is a compromise. One tends to read between the lines of what the Press Secretary tells you and what you have heard elsewhere, and hopefully somewhere in between there's got to be the truth.

What are the limits of reasonable reporting? Do we really need to know if The Queen feeds her eight corgis on fillet steak? Is it of world-shattering importance that the public finds out if it is true that Princess Diana dances alone to disco records in the privacy of Kensington Palace? And do we really have the right to know about all those girls from the Duke of York bachelor days, who sell their stories to the highest bidder? What are the lines of demarcation between responsible royal reporting and intrusion into the private lives of the Royal Family?

There has only been one occasion when The Queen has taken legal action to prevent a story involving a member of her family being published. It happened on 21 February 1983, when the *Sun* printed an exclusive article about the antics of Prince Andrew and his then girl-friend Koo Stark. The story revealed how they lived it up in Buckingham

Palace when The Queen was abroad and how Miss Stark, who, incidentally, has never said one word to the Press about her relationship with the Prince, romped through the corridors and ran barefoot in and out of the State Rooms. It also promised further revelations about the Princess of Wales. The source of the article was a former employee in the Royal Household, who had worked for a little over two years as a junior storeman. Within three weeks of leaving Buckingham Palace he had sold his story to the *Sun* for what was said to be several thousand pounds, in spite of the fact that all employees in royal service sign an undertaking not to disclose any information they might come by during their period of employment. When the story broke, The Queen was en route for the West Coast of America on board the Royal Yacht, and as soon as she was informed, she decided, on the advice of her Private Secretary Sir Philip Moore, to apply for an injunction to prevent any further disclosures. The application was actually made in the name of Mr (now Sir) Russell Wood, the Deputy Treasurer of The Queen's Household, the man who paid the storeman's wages. The injunction was granted and the newspaper in question stopped the offending articles. There was a tremendous amount of coverage given to the case by all the other national newspapers, every one of which seemed to be delighted that one of their competitors had been given this public 'slap on the wrist'. But the *Sun* didn't come out of it too badly either. Even though they had to stop printing the story, the amount of free advertising they received as a result of the action brought by The Queen was worth far more than they would have made if the story had been published. It was an occasion when the Palace decided that the rules of what they regard as decent and responsible reporting had been breached, and they moved swiftly to abort what might have proved to be the birth of a monster. If they had failed to prevent this particular former servant from telling his story, who knows who else might be tempted into revealing the behind-the-scenes gossip at other royal homes? Already Stephen Barry, a former valet to the Prince of Wales, had published a book in America giving intimate details of his time with the heir to the throne. Barry probably became the most famous and certainly the richest defector since 'Crawfie', The Queen's governess, who was the first royal servant to sell her story to the Press. Barry was reported to have made more than a quarter of a million pounds from his book *Royal Service* which was published in America by Macmillan, but so far it has not been published in Britain.

Probably more books have been written about members of the Royal Family than anyone else in the world. In 1981, when Lady Diana Spencer became engaged to the Prince of Wales, no fewer than eighty books were written on her alone. They ranged from tiny children's booklets which had been put together in a matter of weeks to serious, well-researched biographies selling at prices up to £12·95 each.

There are authors who specialise in writing about royalty and a select few are welcome at Buckingham Palace and given remarkable facilities in their research. Elizabeth Longford has written what many people regard as the definitive biography of The Queen – *Elizabeth R*. It contains nearly 500 pages and catalogues in chronological order the life of The Queen, her work and the various aspects of the constitutional monarchy. Lady Longford could not have written the book at all without the utmost co-operation and she acknowledges this in the foreword to her biography. The Queen has never given interviews but both Queen Elizabeth the Queen Mother and Princess Margaret were interviewed by Lady Longford, and there is no doubt that they agreed to this after discussions with The Queen herself; they would not have talked to an author without the permission of Her Majesty. Similarly, Theo Aronson in his book *Royal Family* is able to quote members of the Royal Family and the Household at length. This is because he treats his subject with respect and authority and is not looking for any sensational disclosures.

When I wrote the biography of Princess Anne, I spent many hours with her and members of her staff, both at Buckingham Palace and abroad. After a long period of negotiating, Her Royal Highness had decided that if the book was going to be written anyway, it might as well be factually correct and so she agreed to cooperate. Once that decision had been taken, all the people I wanted to interview were willing to talk to me, but each one checked with the Princess's office first.

There is no such thing as an authorised biography of a living member of the Royal Family. They simply do not give that authority to any one author. But what does occasionally happen is that they will agree to cooperate and the book is then 'approved'. This doesn't mean they have the right of final approval of the manuscript; indeed, they rarely have the opportunity of reading it before publication, but sometimes they will check certain passages to see if they want to add anything or have it deleted if there is an error. Such was the case with my book. The only chapter Princess Anne wanted to see before publication was the one dealing with her equestrian career. I was pleased to send it to Gatcombe Park and she returned it to me with several comments written in her own hand – mainly on the factual details of how many times she had been thrown off and similar points. I was delighted to include these comments because obviously they added a greater authority to my narrative. There was never any attempt by Her Royal Highness or any of her Household to influence me in my opinions.

Douglas Keay is an author who has written a great deal about the Royal

Family. He seems to specialise in articles about the Duke of Edinburgh and judging by the number of personal interviews he has conducted with His Royal Highness, they have obviously built up a mutual trust over the years. He says that, as long as one sticks to the subject agreed, there is no problem. In our BBC Radio series *The Monarchy in Britain* out of which this book came, I asked him if he had to submit lists of questions before he went to Buckingham Palace for a royal interview. This was his answer:

Everybody told me that I would have to submit long lists of questions and even show them the article afterwards, but it hasn't happened that way with me. The first time I interviewed Prince Philip I said 'Presumably you'd like to see this first' and he said 'No', and I went away very disappointed because I thought there can't be anything in it. I've usually outlined the main areas for discussion because obviously you have to set the ground rules, but I think the best way to conduct an interview is to regard it as a conversation, which is what I've always tried to do with the Royal Family. I've found them extremely pleasant to talk to and compared with some other people I've interviewed, such as Mrs Thatcher, they're not difficult.

It is not by any means just the down-market tabloids that print news and views about the Royal Family. Every newspaper in Fleet Street has a correspondent who specialises in royal events, even if the more serious of them are somewhat restrained in what they write. Different publications look for different angles on the royal stories for their readers. Obviously, the people who take *The Times,* the *Telegraph* or the *Guardian* are interested in quite different aspects of royalty from those whose daily intake of news comes via the *Sun*, the *Mirror* and the *Star*. The *Daily Mail* and the *Daily Express* give a great deal of space to royal events, with a wide gap between what their respective royal correspondents write and the items contained in their famous 'gossip columns'. Nigel Dempster who writes the Mail Diary under his own name frequently discloses something the Royal Family would much prefer to keep quiet and he maintains a constant battle with his opposite numbers on the *Express* who contribute to the 'William Hickey' column. They are always looking for the exclusive scoop which will give them an edge over the competition and sometimes they are able to write a story secure in the knowledge that Buckingham Palace rarely issues denials. The two royal correspondents for those papers are highly respected (and highly paid) members of an exclusive group of royal watchers, and while each one would dearly like to scoop the other, they realise that to do their jobs properly, they need the goodwill of the Press Secretary at Buckingham Palace, so they do not allow themselves the freedom of their 'gossip columnist' colleagues.

James Whitaker of the *Daily Mirror* was once asked where he obtained his information, particularly when he writes a story which has obviously come from inside the Palace. He said in reply that he had eleven 'moles' who gave him stories and they ranged from junior members of the domestic staff at various royal homes to senior officials in the Royal Household, and even relatives of the Royal Family themselves. At the lower level, informants receive tip-off fees for good stories, while at the top the remuneration is usually in the form of 'a magnum of Dom Pérignon'. But why should people who are close to the Royal Family take the risk of being discovered – especially if once they are found out it means instant dismissal? Whitaker says it is for a variety of reasons: 'Some feel it is important for the public to know what is going on behind the scenes; others do it for the money, but most of them like to feel they have knowledge that others don't have, it makes them feel important.'

Probably the only journalist who regularly receives a welcome at Buckingham Palace is the Press Association Court Correspondent. This is a unique position and the accreditation is greatly valued and jealously guarded. The Press Association is the news agency which handles all Press Releases from Buckingham Palace and it is the organisation which is called in first whenever there is a major royal story. All announcements of births, marriages, deaths, engagements and appointments are made via the Press Association and the men and one woman who have been their Court Correspondents have all considered themselves to have been in very privileged positions in the world of royal journalism.

The first Press Association Court Correspondent was George Morton-Smith, who served from 1894 until 1927. He became one of the best-known reporters of his day and like one or two others who have had the good fortune to become close to the Royal Family, some of the 'regality' rubbed off. He soon earned the sobriquet 'Royal Smith' – a nickname which stayed with him for the rest of his life. The job must have been popular because each of the first three Court Correspondents remained for more than twenty years and two of them, Louis Wulff, who occupied the post from 1927–50, and Ronnie Gomer Jones, 1950–71, were honoured by the sovereign as MVO and CVO respectively. 'Dougie' Dumbrell was Court Correspondent for only five years, 1972–77, but he became one of the great characters among royal reporters and when he left he too was awarded the MVO. Grania Forbes was the only woman to become Court Correspondent and her sympathetic but straightforward approach to the job earned her tremendous respect, not only from the Press Office at the Palace but among her colleagues in Fleet Street, who haven't always regarded those who write about royal events as being on the same journalistic levels as themselves.

The current Court Correspondent for the Press Association is Tom Corby, who sees himself not as simply the man the Palace calls in when they want something published, but as a genuine newsman, whose job is to seek out the stories the public wants to read. He says:

I am not some sort of substratum courtier. This is strictly a news appointment and my job is to report the news as it affects the Royal Family. It's a great running story. No other country has got a Royal Family quite like ours – two superstars (The Queen and the Princess of Wales) – it's all there. Everybody wants to know about them; they all love to read about them, whether they are pro, anti or luke-warm.

Corby acknowledges that the relationship between himself and The Queen's Press Secretary, Michael Shea, is good and friendly, but even he would like to see what he calls 'a little loosening up on the dividing line on what is private for the Royal Family and what is public'. He feels that if there was this loosening up then more sympathetic stories would be written. He gives an example:

The joint twenty-first-birthday party for Prince Edward and Lady Helen Windsor at Windsor Castle was classified as a private function so there was no facility for *any* Court Correspondent to go in for even half an hour to set the scene. Now that was a nice, warm, sympathetic story of young people enjoying themselves. Half an hour in the room getting the feel of it wouldn't have hurt, but the dividing line is there – and I expect it will always be there.

I have taken up this point with several members of the Royal Family myself and always received the same replies. They feel that when they are attending public functions, the Press has every right to be there – and indeed they would probably be surprised and disappointed if they were not – but when the occasion is private, the Press has no right to be present and accordingly they are given no cooperation. The big question is: what is a private occasion? I asked Princess Anne how she drew the dividing line. She said:

When I am competing at a horse trials that is something from my private life and should be respected as such. I don't object to equestrian reporters being present because they are there because of the event itself and all they are concerned with is the level of performance. But the photographers and reporters who follow me are not interested in the competition as such; what they want is the sensational picture of me falling in the water or having a public row.

She's quite right of course, but perhaps a little ingenuous in believing that when she is competing at a public horse trials, she is not 'fair game'. Editors know all too well that the best pictures and stories come from the unrehearsed occasions and they know their readers want to see and hear about the events that are not announced in the Court Circular.

When the Prince and Princess of Wales went skiing in Switzerland in 1984 they claimed their holiday was ruined through the intrusion of the photographers and reporters who wouldn't leave them alone. The Press said if the Princess would pose for a couple of pictures at the start of the holiday they would leave them alone for the rest of their stay. The Princess refused and the Press corps remained to harass them throughout the vacation. Both had a point. The Princess wanted privacy; the Press wanted stories. Even if the royal couple had posed at the beginning as requested, it is highly unlikely that the photographers would have gone home as promised. None of them was going to miss the chance of a scoop picture of the most photographed young woman in the world. It was an unhappy experience all round and fairly unusual as far as the Princess of Wales was concerned. She is one of the most popular members of the Royal Family with the world's Press and she has happily cooperated on many occasions. Since then the old relationship has in the main been restored, and these days Princess Diana is once again the darling of Fleet Street. Of course she has extraordinary beauty and is uncannily photogenic – she seems unable to be photographed unfavourably.

The Press's favourite royal character is of course Queen Elizabeth the Queen Mother, who can do no wrong in their eyes. She always makes their job as easy as she can and is very aware of how to stand so that photographers can compose the best pictures. Whenever she leaves or enters a building she will pause just long enough for everyone present to capture their favourite shots, and she has been known to wait if she sees one unfortunate photographer who hasn't loaded his film in time. Queen Elizabeth is also aware of how important it is to her and the rest of the Royal Family to have good relations with the media. She is shrewd enough to realise that by getting them on her side, it follows that they will do their best to show her in a favourable light. So both sides are professional in their approach to their jobs, and each respects the other's point of view.

Nothing has brought the monarchy to the attention of the world as much as television. The BBC and ITV both have Court Correspondents who are accredited to Buckingham Palace and they accompany The Queen on every State Visit overseas, reporting back the trivial as well as the important aspects of the tour. If they can find something off-beat to report, so much the better. The two main broadcasting organisations take their royal coverage very seriously and monitor each other's programmes to see if one has received more cooperation and better facilities from the Palace than the other. Today nearly every major State occasion is seen through the lenses of the cameras placed at strategic points inside the royal palaces and along the processional routes. The public has become as familiar with the sight of The Queen and her Family at banquets, opening Parliament and attending weddings and other services at Westminster Abbey and St Paul's Cathedral, as they have with the daily happenings at *Coronation Street* and *Crossroads*.

Despite her initial apprehension over the televising of her coronation (see page 83), The Queen has always been in favour of having State occasions filmed and broadcast live. Television (and, more recently, international transmission by satellite) has played a vital part in portraying the splendour and ceremonial of the monarchy and its value is fully realised by The Queen and her advisers. Certainly the extent of the coverage is now vast: the wedding of Prince Andrew and Miss Sarah Ferguson in July 1986 was seen by an estimated world-wide audience of 1000 million people.

Each time a royal wedding or other State occasion has been seen on television (and since The Queen's coronation in 1953, every royal wedding, funeral and anniversary service has been), it is with the express permission of The Queen who is advised on each stage of the proceedings by her Press Secretary Michael Shea, and of course by the man who is credited with making the biggest changes in the attitude of the Palace to the media, the present Private Secretary, Sir William Heseltine. This affable, extremely efficient Australian arrived at Buckingham Palace in the sixties as a temporary assistant to Commander Colville in the Press Office. Heseltine was a man who understood the Press and who was able to really communicate with them. On a difficult foreign tour he could explain, over a pint of beer, the problems his employers were having and also, when he saw The Queen at her daily briefings, try to relate the difficulties the Press were experiencing in doing their jobs. It was the start of a new era in Buckingham Palace public and Press relations, and apart from the odd hiccup, things have never looked back since then.

The biggest single breakthrough as far as the public image of the monarchy is concerned was achieved in 1969. Again it was Bill Heseltine who was mainly responsible. The BBC had decided they would like to film a year in the life of the Royal Family. They wanted their cameras to capture every moment, public and private, above and below stairs, showing aspects of The Queen and her Family that had never been seen before – and maybe never would again. In Commander Colville's time such a programme would have been unthinkable and the suggestion would not even have been put before The Queen, let alone been given serious consideration. But Bill Heseltine, by now Her Majesty's Press Secretary, realised that this was a golden opportunity of showing the Royal Family as a warm, modern, caring group of people who were very much a family of the times, and not some outmoded anachronism living in an ivory tower. He persuaded The Queen to agree to all the BBC's requests and the resulting film, which was shown all over the world, was an outstanding success. The Duke of Edinburgh had a private view of the film before any other members of the Family and his job was to report back to The Queen anything he thought should be edited out. The producer Richard Cawston, who was to become one of The Queen's favourite producers and looked after Her Majesty's annual Christmas message for many years, was naturally more than a little apprehensive at the prospect of showing the film to his royal one-man audience. But he needed to have no fears; the Duke was delighted with the finished product and when The Queen saw it, she too realised that Bill Heseltine had been right. From that day on, the image of the Royal Family changed completely from the one previously held by the majority of people. The programme, called *Royal Family*, set the standard for all future television coverage and allowed the BBC and ITV unprecedented entrée on royal occasions in the years to come.

My own experience in working with members of the Royal Family began in 1971 when I was a reporter with BBC Television News. Princess Anne was competing at Burghley in the European Three-Day-Event Championships and by the final Sunday she was in the lead. My editor sent me with a film crew to see if she would be interviewed in the event that she won. History has recorded that, at the age of twenty-one, she became European Champion. She received the Raleigh Trophy from her mother and was ready to talk about her plans for the future. In those days Buckingham Palace Press Secretaries did not accompany junior members of the Royal Family and the only person with her was the Crown Equerry, Sir John Miller. I approached him and enquired if he would mind asking the Princess if she would answer a few questions. She agreed immediately and we began filming. The BBC producer of the Outside Broadcast unit responsible for the riding events was furious at being 'scooped' by News, but of course I was delighted because my interview was shown all over the world. There was a pleasant sequel to this incident. Some weeks later I received a letter from Bill Heseltine saying that the Princess had been so busy on the day in question that she had not even seen her final round and the television interview, so would we oblige and let them have a private view? The BBC promptly assembled a compilation of Princess Anne's three days plus the interview, which I then took to Buckingham Palace. A short time later I received a delightful letter from the Princess thanking me for my efforts and for the present of the film. Since then I have interviewed Her Royal Highness on several occasions, including the official engagement interview at Buckingham Palace, and much more informal chats at Gatcombe Park. It culminated in a television programme about her working life for which I and the camera crew spent a year following her around. She was the most cooperative subject I have worked with: totally professional and extremely knowledgeable about the requirements of the director. She agreed to nearly every suggestion we made and I was welcomed at her home whenever I needed to talk to her; even on one occasion when she had just had two injections shortly before flying off to India for the Save the Children Fund. So obviously I have a slight bias towards the Princess – and so, if they are honest, do the rest of our team. When the filming was complete, the Princess arranged for all of us and our families to attend a Garden Party at Buckingham Palace, and she went out of her way to meet and talk to the wives of the crew; not the action of a stuck-up, arrogant lady.

Documentary programmes have since been made about the Prince and Princess of Wales, Captain Mark Phillips, and Prince Andrew; probably the most successful of all was *Royal Heritage* in which the late Sir Huw Wheldon guided viewers through the treasures of the Royal Collection. Made originally in 1976, the book of the series became a best-seller, earning for Wheldon more than half a million pounds, and the series was repeated with equal success again in 1986.

Whenever a television programme is planned by the BBC or ITV in Britain, there is a set routine which has to be followed. No producer or writer is allowed direct access to the Palace without first going through the official Palace liaison officers that both organisations employ. Cliff Morgan, an ebullient, former Welsh rugby international is Head of Outside Broadcasts at the BBC and as such is responsible for all royal broadcasting on radio and television. His office looks after all requests for interviews with members of the Royal Family and programmes involving royalty. He supervises (with just one assistant, Jane Astell) The Queen's Christmas message, the State Opening of Parliament, all royal weddings, funerals, Royal Ascot, the Royal Maundy Service and anything else that might occur, while he also controls Match of the Day, Wimbledon, the Cup Final and every other sporting event covered by the BBC. If a producer wants to make a programme about the Royal Family, he or she will first of all write to Cliff Morgan, giving as many details as possible about the proposal. This is then forwarded to Michael Shea at Buckingham Palace for further consideration. If the project is considered in the best interests of the Royal Family – and this is the only criterion – the producer will be invited to the Palace for a talk. Then follow many more detailed discussions about what is and is not allowed and eventually the programme is made. The Palace sometimes impose certain conditions on the making of a programme: they will want to see the finished production before it is transmitted so that any changes they want can be made; they will decide which part of the subject's lifestyle can be shown on television and which parts remain strictly 'off limits'. Occasionally there is a financial agreement in which part of the proceeds is given to a charity nominated by the particular member of the Royal Family who is taking part in the programme.

This all sounds as if there is a great deal of interference with the editorial control. There isn't. Once the details have been agreed, directors are left to get on with it in their own way. When we were making the Princess Anne film, we didn't see anyone from the Press Office throughout the entire year we were filming. Nevertheless, one is always aware that what is considered an urgent priority by the television company is not necessarily thought of in the same light by the Palace.

As far as Indepenent Television is concerned, the liaison between the Palace and all the ITV companies is left in the hands of Ronald Allison of Thames Television Ltd. During the five years he worked as The Queen's Press Secretary, he became not only one of the Royal Family's favourite servants but was also held in high regard by his former colleagues at the BBC, for whom he was Court Correspondent for many years. He obviously has a unique insight into the way the Palace works, so his advice is invaluable when producers want to know what is likely to receive approval. On special royal occasions he is able to bring a personal note into the commentary which, of course, other broadcasters cannot do.

As Michael Shea has been quoted as saying, it is a common myth among editors in Fleet Street that the Royal Family needs them more than they need the Royal Family. Perhaps a more realistic assessment would be that both need each other. We live in a world where not only the Royal Family, but holders of high office throughout the world have to be seen to be doing their jobs. There needs to be a line of communication to the ordinary reader and viewer of television. The difficult task of the image-makers – and the Palace Press Office is as much in the business of creating an image as any commercial public relations company – is to keep control, so that a balanced view is presented. It is alright to let in a little bit of daylight from time to time, but the mystery must be maintained. The Queen may be the most human of human beings but she is not like the rest of us. She is the sovereign and as such must always remain apart, in spite of the so-called 'democratisation of the monarchy', as some observers describe the process by which the Royal Family has become more accessible to the public and Press. It is patently ridiculous for newspaper editors and reporters to say that were it not for them the monarchy would disappear, but at the same time the Royal Family has a real need for the media. They would find it very odd if, on a foreign tour, there was not a cloud of cameras and reporters trailing behind them, and equally odd if a week passed by without one of them appearing on our television screens.

The voracious appetite of a public ever hungry for scraps of news from the royal table is in no danger of being satisfied, and if the Royal Family didn't feel the need to feed items about themselves from time to time, they would have no use for a Press Office. The monarchy has never been as popular as it is today, partly because of the person who occupies the throne, and partly because of the skilful exploitation of the media by one of the most successful public relations machines in the world.

Michael Shea was replaced by Robin Janvrin, as Press Secretary to The Queen, in June, 1987, and Victor Chapman, one of the Assistant Press Secretaries, returned to Canada in October, 1987. He was succeeded by a Scottish journalist, Philip Mackie.

CONCLUSION

Nobody, not even the most ardent royalist, has ever claimed that monarchy is cheap. By virtue of the fact that the sovereign is regarded as being apart from the rest of the people, and should be seen to be so, it follows that the monarchy has to be maintained in a manner both regal and expensive. This does not mean that it is necessarily more expensive than maintaining an elected official: in America the cost of the upkeep of the White House and the Presidency is far greater than the combined cost of maintaining the entire British Royal Family and the Prime Minister.

Nevertheless it has long been a bone of contention that The Queen and her Family are costing the British taxpayers too much money. It is true that the entire cost of the monarchy is borne by the British Government (Commonwealth countries pay nothing) but it has also been argued that the country actually makes a profit out of the Royal Family, if we take into consideration the income that derives from such 'invisible' earnings as tourism. It is impossible to estimate the amount of money the Royal Family attracts into Britain via the tourist industry, but the British Tourist Authority say that The Queen and her Family and the royal residences are the number one attractions for visitors from all over the world, and the sums involved must be in the tens of millions of pounds. It has also been suggested that if the Crown decided to keep all the income from the land, office buildings, shops, houses, farms, quarries, mines and mineral rights it owns and hand back to the government the money it receives under the Civil List, the Crown would have the better of the deal. It might be argued that such income would be taxed; not necessarily, since revenue from Crown lands has always been tax-free. So by the process of simple arithmetic it is possible to work out that, far from costing the taxpayers a great deal of unnecessary expense, the Royal Family actually contributes a lot of money to the country. Even when taking into account the extraordinary payments for refitting the Royal Yacht, The Queen's Flight and the Royal Train, there is still a balance in favour of the Treasury.

In all the arguments put forward against the monarchy during the past thirty years, there has rarely been a single accusation levelled at The Queen personally. Even the most ardent republicans have admitted that the present occupant of the throne is a dedicated, hard-working and conscientious sovereign, with a genuine love of her people and an unequalled sense

145

of duty. The arguments have been about whether the institution of monarchy should be allowed to continue – either in its present form or in a more modified version. There have been many reasoned discussions on the worth of such an institution in the latter part of the twentieth century, as well as extreme condemnations of the extravagant lifestyles of The Queen and her Family. Some of the better reasons for abolishing the monarchy have in fact been put, unintentionally, by its most devoted followers, who have made claims on behalf of the monarchy which could only be justified in a deity.

The late Richard Crossman once wrote: 'The myths and legends of a monarchy are only credible to the masses so long as those who propagate them believe in their own propaganda. What gives the British monarchy its unique strength is the fact that the Court, the aristocracy and the Church – not to mention the middle classes – are just as credulous worshippers of it as the masses.' It was Crossman who once asked if he could be excused attending the State Opening of Parliament because he felt the ceremonial was outmoded and pointless. A senior member of the Royal Household put it to him that perhaps there were occasions when The Queen did not feel like attending such ceremonies, but nevertheless she felt it her duty to do so. Crossman withdrew his objections and turned up.

The most often quoted criticism of the monarchy is the one made famous by Lord Altrincham in 1957. In an edition of the *National & English Review*, which he both owned and edited, he wrote about The Queen's entourage as being 'stuffy and tweedy' and Her Majesty's style of speaking as a 'pain in the neck'. It was the first major criticism directed at The Queen herself and immediately started an uproar. The vast majority of the people 'demanded his head' while a vocal minority felt that he had said much that was true and needed to be said. The left-wing Member of Parliament Willie Hamilton has made frequent attacks on the Royal Family and can be relied upon to provide headlines whenever the subject of royal finances is aired. He has also done rather well himself out of his books and other writing on the Royal Family. In 1977 (Jubilee year) Mr Hamilton contributed to a Penguin anthology called *The Queen*, saying:

For twenty-five years, HM Queen Elizabeth II has sat on a throne surrounded by a morass of disillusion, decadence and decay. In the course of her reign the Queen has seen seven different Prime Ministers come and go . . . whatever advice, warning or encouragement she may have given them, the nation's problems have worsened rather than improved. The new Elizabethan era which was trumpeted in with such absurd romanticism twenty-five years ago has gone sour.

On the cost of the monarchy, Hamilton is just as damning saying:

No one can know the real cost in money terms . . . Royal finances are tangled in the cobwebs of history. The story is a mixture of scarcely concealed royal greed and increasing public expenditure. . . . That the Queen is one of the wealthiest women in the world there can be no doubt. That wealth has been accumulated by a combination of shrewdness and sound business advice from city gentlemen, but above all by priceless tax privileges not available to any of her subjects.

In summarising his case against the monarchy, Willie Hamilton says:

For my part, the case for a democratically elected head of state, a President, is unanswerable. The case for the continued existence of an hereditary monarch is as weak and indefensible as that for retaining a predominantly hereditary House of Lords. It is a hangover from feudal times. It serves no useful purpose. To those who want to see fundamental changes in the nature of our society, it is an impediment which must be abolished.

Lord Soper, a staunch republican and advocate of the abolition of the monarchy, is another who feels we do not *need* a monarch but he also says that the comparative simplicity of that statement conceals a much more profound and complicated issue. People need to personalise the environment in which they live and in that respect they like to think of somebody who represents the best of conditions that they themselves would like to enjoy. His objection to the monarchy is the assumption of power rather than representation. He says, 'I can't subscribe to the idea that we need somebody who is to have the kind of authority that monarchy suggests. The kind of leadership I would like to see is not the leadership of either superstition or hereditary, but the leadership which does represent, among ordinary people, the kind of life they would like to follow themselves.'

Those who argue for the retention of the monarchy in its present form include prominent politicians of every party, with Lord Wilson of Rievaulx acting as spokesman when he said: 'The fact that there is somebody different, separate and uncommitted, whose only concern is to see that Parliament and Government reflect the decisions of her people, is something one just doesn't have in presidential states, and that is one of the great advantages that Britain has.'

Even some of those to whom the holding of any hereditary title or office is intolerable find reasons to exclude the monarchy from their general calls for abolition. Many people truly believe that it is the monarchy which holds Britain together and the continuous line of which Elizabeth II is the present representative is the one thing that distinguishes the United Kingdom from being a 'banana republic'.

What are the realities? Does the monarchy underpin a class-conscious nation living in the past? In a country in which less than a tenth of the adult population regularly attend church or chapel, is there any need for a

Defender of the Faith and do we get the spiritual leadership which that title indicates? Is the monarchy interested only in its own survival? Would Britain be any worse off if there was no monarchy?

Whether or not we would be worse off under a president is almost impossible to quantify; the facts speak for themselves regarding the feeling of the general public for the Royal Family. Nobody attracts such public acclaim as The Queen. During her tour of Britain in 1977, Jubilee Year, it was estimated that more than half the total population turned out to greet her. The wedding of the Prince and Princess of Wales in 1981 was watched by 500 million people throughout the world with 100,000 lining the streets of London to see the royal processions in person. The same fervour happened again in 1986 when the Duke of York married Miss Sarah Ferguson. What is the attraction? Would as many people turn out if the leading players were television or film stars? Do we simply need heroes, no matter who they are, or is there something special about the British Royal Family?

If popularity is a yardstick by which we can measure the success or otherwise of the monarchy in Britain, the arguments are already won. Numerous polls held since The Queen acceded to the throne in 1952 have all indicated that the monarchy is the institution which enjoys more public support than any other. In fact, in the thirty-four years The Queen has reigned its prestige has been enhanced almost beyond measure. When Her Majesty became Queen she was little known outside the United Kingdom, other than as the daughter of King George VI. At the age of twenty-five she had had virtually no experience of world affairs and her first Prime Minister Winston Churchill was naturally apprehensive about having to deal with someone half a century younger than he was himself. There was a great deal more than the normal generation gap: he had been born in Victorian times with the values and manners of that era. His new sovereign was an untried, inexperienced young woman with two very young children and she was becoming Head of State at a time when Britain's prestige as a major power was heading into a serious decline. Churchill's fears were quickly allayed and within months he was to speak publicly about his admiration for the way in which The Queen had grasped the essential ingredients of Britain's new role; not as the centre of an empire but as the focal point for a new Commonwealth.

Britain's decline as an industrial nation and a world power may well have continued throughout the reign of The Queen but while the reputation of the country has diminished, the prestige of the monarchy has increased enormously. To many other countries throughout the world the British monarchy is one of the few things which still commands respect and admiration. It may well be that the leaders of the forty-nine

Commonwealth countries have their own pragmatic reasons for continuing to belong to an organisation which has its headquarters in the country which was once the heart of the colonial empire. Certainly it cannot be just because they like Britain, or because they somehow feel a loyalty to a country which has at some time put most of them in jail when they were fighting for independence. There is something else, apart from the practical benefits, which makes them want to be part of this family of nations and that something is the monarchy itself – or perhaps more particularly the person who is monarch at the present time. Each Commonwealth leader enjoys a special relationship with The Queen, one which would be impossible with another President or Prime Minister. The magic of the monarchy sets The Queen apart from, and above, politics and her vast experience as Head of the Commonwealth has made her unique as the linchpin of this extraordinary collection of 900 million people of different races and cultures. In 1986 there was a real danger that the Commonwealth would disintegrate over the question of the British Government's refusal to approve sanctions against South Africa. Zambia had threatened to pull out and if that had happened it was likely that other African countries would have followed. The Commonwealth would have fallen apart. The threat was in fact averted, but not before the Commonwealth Games in Edinburgh had been devastated by the withdrawal of more than twenty countries in protest. A meeting was held in London and afterwards a private dinner party was given at Buckingham Palace by The Queen. She spoke individually with each of the leaders present and the talk of leaving the Commonwealth disappeared. President Kaunda of Zambia says no other person in the world commands such respect and affection as The Queen of England and one of the most important ways she shows her feelings for her people is the way she treats them all equally. There are no special favourites – or if there are Her Majesty never shows it. That is perhaps the most significant aspect of the monarchy in this democratic age; the fact that The Queen does not make any distinctions between her subjects. The Court may still be populated by members of the most aristocratic families in the land (though even this is changing with the introduction of 'professionals' into the Royal Household) but as far as The Queen is concerned they, and we, are all the same to her. There is a common misunderstanding that because The Queen surrounds herself with Ladies-in-Waiting who all come from similar upper-class backgrounds, and courtiers whose pedigrees are very nearly as long as her own, she is part of their social category. It is of course a complete fallacy. The Royal Family is in a social category entirely its own. I have met The Queen, the Duke of Edinburgh, the Prince and Princess of Wales, the Duke of York, Prince Edward, Princess Anne and her husband a number of times, in a variety of situations, and they have greeted me and spoken to me in exactly the same way as they greet the Archbishop of Canterbury or the Duke of Norfolk. I have watched The Queen talking to old ladies in London's East End and there is not the slightest hint of condescension in her manner. I have also seen her with some of her oldest friends. Her attitude is the same; it is ours that changes. The monarchy is a great leveller which reduces everybody else to the same rank. The same applies with politics. Many people assume that, because of who she is, The Queen is more likely to be a Conservative than a Socialist and would consequently be more at home with Conservative ministers than Labour. There has never been any evidence to support this theory; in fact, if the accounts given by a number of the eight Prime Ministers who have served The Queen are considered, the opposite seems to be the case. Both Harold Wilson and James Callaghan enjoyed an extremely close working relationship with Her Majesty, while some former Conservative Prime Ministers appear to have been unable to establish a rapport. In the Penguin anthology *The Queen* Peregrine Worsthorne wrote that:

> . . . it is the essence of monarchy that all ranks hold it in equal awe, are equally its servants, and this applies to the great figures of the democracy as well as the great figures of the aristocracy. Precisely because it is an institution resting on a principle or concept separate from, and superior to, the sources of all other forms of secular power, it can and does subdue every form of pride and arrogance: the pride and arrogance of elected power as much as the pride and arrogance of wealth or the pride and arrogance of lineage, or even the pride and arrogance of churches. The Prime Minister, the head of the civil service, the Earl Marshal, the chairman of the largest corporation, the governor of the Bank of England, the Archbishop all bow before the throne, as low as the meanest, poorest, humblest in the land.

In theory the powers of the monarchy are awesome. The sovereign could sell all the ships in the navy, disband the army and give away as much or as little of her territory as she pleases. In practice, of course, she could do none of these things. She reigns but does not rule. The Victorian writer Walter Bagehot wrote a masterly summary of the position of the monarchy and the constitution in 1867 when he defined the three major rights of the sovereign as: 'The right to be consulted, the right to encourage, the right to warn.' These are still the most often quoted lines from Bagehot's essay and are regarded as being as true today as they were more than a hundred years ago. Queen Victoria felt she had one more right: the right to interfere, which she frequently did, sometimes to an extent that her Government would not tolerate. Our present Queen exercises those three rights today in the way she uses her influence if not her actual power. The influence of the monarchy is the essential ingredient contained in the function of the Crown. Because The Queen is the most experienced Head of State in the world, it follows that her advice to her Prime Minister would rarely if ever be disregarded. This is the manner in which Her Majesty can 'warn' her politicians today. As far as the actual power of the Crown is concerned this is slightly more difficult to define. The Royal Assent is necessary before Parliamentary Acts can become legal, but The Queen cannot withhold that assent. She acts on the advice of a minister of the Crown in almost every case but 'advice' really means instruction. If The Queen were to decide not to give the Royal Assent to a piece of legislation it would mean a constitutional crisis, ending in either the dissolution of Parliament or the end of the monarchy. The principle of the sovereign acting only on the advice of her ministers is beneficial to both parties in that the Prime Minister of the day is able to carry out the wishes of the elected government and at the same time protect the sovereign from parliamentary and public criticism. Of course not all the 'advice' The Queen receives comes from the British Government. In those Commonwealth countries where Her Majesty is represented by a Governor-General there is a direct channel of communication to the sovereign; the British Government is not involved in any way. The most significant example of this was during the Australian constitutional crisis in 1975 when the then Governor-General Sir John Kerr dismissed the Prime Minister, Mr Gough Whitlam. Sir John had acted on his own initiative, which he was legally entitled to do, keeping The Queen informed of his actions through her Private Secretary, but without communicating with the British Government at all.

The only power the sovereign has in the political context is in the appointment of the Prime Minister. The Queen has individual responsibility for sending for the man or woman whose party commands a majority in the House of Commons, but she does not have to act on the 'advice' of the outgoing Prime Minister, or anyone else for that matter. If The Queen needs to consult about the appointment of a new Prime Minister, the advice she may receive is exactly that; advice and no more. There has been a great deal of speculation about the method The Queen will use in appointing a Prime Minister if there is a 'hung Parliament' at the next General Election. If such a situation arises Her Majesty will have to exercise her discretion in the appointment. Her Private Secretary will play an important role because of his connections with the leaders of all political parties and his knowledge of the mood of the people and Parliament. No doubt The Queen will call on other senior statesmen, former Prime Ministers and authorities on the constitution, but the final decision will be hers and hers alone. It is in situations like these that the value of having someone above the reach of party politics is best displayed. A President would be known to be of a particular political leaning – no one really knows how The Queen would vote if she were eligible.

Another of the powers of the sovereign is the right to dismiss the Prime Minister and dissolve Parliament. No sovereign, however, has dismissed a Prime Minister since William IV discharged Lord Melbourne in 1834 and it is unlikely that any monarch in the future would repeat his action. What is important is that the monarch should retain this power. As Lord Blake, one of the country's foremost authorities on the monarchy and the constitution, has said: 'The Queen is the guardian of constitutional legitimacy in the broadest sense of the words. She cannot be this without possessing, in addition to influence and prestige however great, some ultimate powers of last resort.'

Britain's monarchy is unique in that, unlike the remaining European monarchies, it has not become in the least democratic in the real sense of the word. The minor royals earn their living in the commercial world, it's true, but the immediate members of the Royal Family remain above such everyday, mundane tasks. No one expects the Duke of Edinburgh or the Prince of Wales to get a job or accept directorships and the idea of The Queen being associated with any business enterprise is as unthinkable today as it would have been a hundred years ago. Apart from the dramatic events of 1936 there is no tradition of abdication, as for example there has been recently in the Royal House of The Netherlands, where two queens have abdicated in favour of daughters. In Spain the King attends meetings of his Cabinet; in Sweden the monarch has lost the right to appoint Prime Ministers. In Norway the Royal Family travels by public transport while in Belgium the King has a job. The magic of Britain's monarchy is such that they do not have to explain their actions to anyone. They are expected to live in grand palaces; travel in isolated splendour and appear in glittering ceremonial wearing crowns and decorations, diamonds and ermine. There may be an awareness of the realities of the modern world but the British people apparently do not want their Royal Family to be seen to be part of it. Lord Blake believes that in preserving its monarchy Britain has also been saved from the possibility of a dictatorship. He adds that a recent survey on the constitutional position of the sovereign showed that a substantial majority believed that if the views of The Queen were seen to be in conflict with those of her Prime Minister, The Queen's opinion would prevail and that it should prevail. However, Lord Blake goes on to say that in a sense we do not need a monarch at all: 'It is not a necessary feature of a western type of modern democracy, but of course it is long established in Britain and the public at large would be very disappointed if we changed over from a monarchy to a republic.'

One of the more balanced political voices to be heard on the subject is that of Austin Mitchell, a Labour Member of Parliament for a Grimsby constituency. He considers the monarchy to be simply a fact of British life, saying:

We've got it, it works and there is no argument for getting rid of it. The continuity is a great thing, in that if we had an elected president it always becomes the subject of party politics and therefore less attractive and popular. But the danger is that monarchy becomes an escapism factor with the people. On the whole I think the continuity of the monarchy is one of its most important characteristics because the whole position of Head of State is important. The main function of the monarchy is as a symbol of unity.

Mr Mitchell, however, does have certain reservations, mainly about the amount of money being spent on maintaining the Royal Family – money which he feels could be put to far better use for a wider good. 'I think the monarchy is inordinately expensive . . . If we had a monarchy which functioned in a much more Scandinavian fashion, symbolic of a more egalitarian society, it would be far healthier for the long-term continuity of the monarchy.' But he too is realistic about the chances of the monarchy disappearing in the foreseeable future, saying:

If there was a vote in Parliament today on whether we should abolish the monarchy I know it would be defeated by an enormous majority. There is a tremendous feeling for The Queen throughout the country and politicians of every party, with very few exceptions, would support the continuance of the monarchy – even if privately they belong to the anti-royalist lobby.

The arguments for and against the monarchy will continue for many years to come. Perhaps they will never be resolved. There are those who would gladly lay down their lives for The Queen, and those who would just as happily lead the parade down The Mall to take over Buckingham Palace in the name of republicanism. Those who argue for the abolition of the monarchy are by no means all 'rebel-rousing' fanatics whose war cry is 'Up the revolution'. Many are sincere, learned men and women with an earnest desire to see what they regard as an outdated, unnecessary institution make way for a more modern, democratic way of selecting a Head of State. And the pro-royalist lobby is as equally divided into unquestioning supporters whose motto is 'Queen and Country' – in that order, no matter who is on the throne – and the serious scholars and students of history who genuinely believe The Queen and her Family reign by divine and legal right. Within the Royal Family itself the principle of hereditary monarchy is accepted without question, which is why the idea of abdication remains unacceptable. Sovereignty is a sacred trust and the person who has been anointed at a coronation remains sovereign for life. Prince Charles knows that he will be king one day and that he will remain on the throne until the day he dies and he also knows that his son William will one day succeed him to become king sometime in the twenty-first century. It is because of this family continuity that Britain's monarchy has lasted for a thousand years. In that time it has rarely been more popular than it is today and in the eyes of many of her subjects, Elizabeth II has given her people more than enough proof that, in Britain at least, monarchy is the most acceptable system for providing a Head of State.

♔ ACKNOWLEDGEMENTS

In writing a book of this nature – and preparing the radio series which preceded it – one inevitably relies to a great extent on a large number of people. Several Members of the Royal Household were unstinting in their help and cooperation and I am glad to record my grateful thanks to all those who took part. When the idea of the radio series was first proposed I received much encouragement and practical assistance from Michael Shea, The Queen's Press Secretary, and John Haslam, Assistant Press Secretary. They arranged interviews with a number of senior Members of the Household, including Rear Admiral Sir Paul Greening (now Master of the Household, then Flag Officer Royal Yachts) and Air Vice-Marshal John de Severne, MVO, OBE, AFC (Captain of The Queen's Flight), as well as members of their respective units.

Sir Oliver Millar (Surveyor of The Queen's Pictures) and Oliver Everett (Librarian at Windsor Castle), gave generously of their time and expertise and Brigadier Kenneth Mears (Deputy Governor, the Tower of London), was equally generous when I visited him at the Tower to see the Crown Jewels.

I would like to place on record a very special appreciation of the help given by Lt.-Col. Sir John Johnston, KCVO, MC, Comptroller of the Lord Chamberlain's Office, St James's Palace. Without his expert knowledge, the chapter on the Royal Household would have looked very different indeed!

A large number of journalists and other 'Royal watchers' contributed, including James Whitaker, Douglas Keay, Godfrey Talbot, Tom Corby, Lynn Bell, Grania Forbes and Ronald Allison. The Archbishop of Canterbury kindly saw me on more than one occasion and the Secretary-General of the Commonwealth, Sir 'Sonny' Ramphal, gave a unique insight into the relationship between The Queen and the Commonwealth countries.

In the discussion on the arguments for and against the monarchy, I was delighted to be able to call on the talents of Austin Mitchell MP, Lord Soper and Lord Blake. I am also indebted to Sir Cenydd Traherne for his description of the installation ceremony of a Knight of the Garter.

My thanks to Dewi Smith and Christine Cadenne of the BBC for their patience and enthusiasm during the making of the radio programmes and

155

to Talia Rodgers at BBC Books for her tactful editing of the manuscript. Sarah Wergan researched the pictures, Ann Thompson was the designer, and, finally, many thanks to Sheila Ableman, who was responsible for the idea of the book in the first place.

Brian Hoey
December 1986

INDEX